THE SCHOOL OF
Chocolate

EQUIPMENT, TECHNIQUES, RECIPES & STEP-BY-STEP INSTRUCTIONS

Francesca Badi & Omar Busi

SIMON &
SCHUSTER
ILLUSTRATED

London · New York · Sydney · Toronto

A CBS COMPANY

English language edition published in Great Britain by Simon & Schuster UK Ltd, 2011
A CBS COMPANY

Published originally under the title 'Scuola di Cioccolato'
© 2009 Food Editore, an imprint of Food S.R.L
Via Mazzini n.6 43121 Parma (www.gruppofood.com)

The right of Francesca Badi and Omar Busi to be identified as authors
of this work has been asserted by them in accordance with sections
77 and 78 of the Copyright, Designs and Patents Act, 1988.

1 3 5 7 9 10 8 6 4 2

SIMON & SCHUSTER ILLUSTRATED BOOKS
Simon & Schuster UK
222 Gray's Inn Road
London WC1X 8HB

www.simonandschuster.co.uk

Simon & Schuster Australia, Sydney

Photographs by Davide Di Prato
Original design: Cristiana Mistrali
Design for the English language edition: Richard Proctor
Recipes by Omar Busi, Licia Cagnoni, Piero Rainone, Simone Rugiati
Contributors: Daniela Beati, Cristina Bottari, Giacomo Gazzola, Chiara Gianferrari,
Giusy Giuffrida, Gino Marazzini, Daniela Martini, Monica Nastrucci

Translated by Sara Harris and Anna Bennett
Copy editor English language: Beverly Davies

A CIP catalogue record for this book is available from the British Library

ISBN 978-0-85720-264-2

Colour reproduction by Dot Gradations Ltd, UK
Printed and bound in China

Recipe notes:
Eggs: All recipes in this book refer to medium eggs. Pregnant women,
the elderly, those in poor health and children should avoid eggs that
are not fully cooked or raw.
Butter: All recipes refer to unsalted butter.
Sugar: All recipes refer to caster sugar, unless otherwise stated.
Flour: '00' flour is recommended for recipes specifying plain flour.

Chocolate is the food of the gods,
a slightly guilty pleasure — who doesn't
enjoy being a little sinful now and again?
It is only a minor transgression and a
healthy one at that. Chocolate is not meant to
satisfy your hunger but, once tasted, the urge
to taste it again is bound to stay with you.

Contents

Chocolate... what a passion!

'I could not take my mouth away from the delicious edges of the cup. Hot chocolate to die for, soft, velvety, fragranced, intoxicating.'

Guy de Maupassant

Who doesn't love chocolate? As an anonymous source says: 'Nine people out of ten love chocolate. The tenth person is lying.' How true! For most people chocolate represents the ultimate self-indulgence, the most irresistible confections which we cannot refuse even if we are on a strict diet. This is what we choose when we want to spoil ourselves after a bad day, or to boost our morale and energy levels before confronting a difficult task.

We had the idea of turning the passion most of us share for this foodstuff into a book with an easy-to-follow patisserie course and a collection of recipes to show the reader how to deal with chocolate in its many forms.

We consulted Omar Busi, a well-known *pâtissier* who specialises in the art of chocolate, and together we formulated a 'patisserie school on paper' in order to guide chocolate lovers towards a knowledge of how to make their own chocolate creations.

In the first part of this book you will start learning *all about chocolate*, how and with which utensils you can prepare basic mixtures, choux pastries, ganaches, mousses, fillings and toppings. At the beginning of this section we tell you what equipment you will need, and provide you with a series of step-by-step instructions on how to use and store two products that are absolutely fundamental in patisserie: vanilla sugar and the sweet 'flour' that is made by mixing together ground almonds and caster sugar.

In the second part of this book, you can indulge your sweet tooth by trying out recipes for chocolate-based cakes, biscuits and confectionery, most of which can be enjoyed throughout the day: at *breakfast-time and beyond*, during your *coffee break*, for *desserts and after-dinner treats* and... for those moments when both body and mind yearn for a little taste of *chocolate heaven*.

As we compiled the recipes, photographed the step-by-step lessons and were told all sorts of culinary secrets, Omar gradually revealed how his passion for chocolate was born and how it continued to grow.

'The greatest tragedies were written by the Greeks and by Shakespeare. Neither knew chocolate.' Sandra Boynton

Omar says

'I was born with a flair for all things technical. For years after leaving university I had a desk job but I felt that I was not really fulfilled: I needed an artistic outlet. I finally discovered what was to be my life's work when I realised that I had never listened to what my inner voice was telling me; no one had thought to suggest where my true talents might lie.

I started to put my artistic talents to the test in patisserie and went on to specialise in working with chocolate. Over the years I learned to love the artistic potential of chocolate creations. I took part in a number of competitions. This awoke a passion for experimenting with all sorts of other ingredients that might combine successfully with chocolate. This lead to collaboration with various companies, which inspired me to deepen my knowledge of this field. Chocolate increasingly began to dominate my professional life until it eventually became its most important facet.

Chocolate is the food of the gods, a delicious indulgence, perhaps even a slightly guilty one, but who doesn't enjoy being a little sin now and again? It is only a minor transgression and when enjoyed in moderation can only do us good. I am a great believer in single portions, small treats, a biscuit or two: chocolate is not meant to satisfy hunger. Having tasted it once, the urge to buy it and taste it the following day and the day after that should remain with you.

Precision and practice

Chocolate is quite beautiful to behold, as well as to taste, but it can also be difficult to work with. It calls for perseverance and concentration. For the best results, you have to be scrupulous in following precise rules on temperature, cooking times, resting times and quantities. The main thing is not to give in to discouragement. When joining our chocolate school all you need is a willingness to be accurate, some determination and plenty of patience.

Just follow the basic rules for working with chocolate: for example, tempering chocolate is a very important process that has to be carried out

almost scientifically in order to make successful chocolate creations and decorations. Many professionals give up working with chocolate because they do not get good results but this is a great pity: you can and will master it!

When I started out I knew absolutely nothing; I studied books, carried out a great deal of research and experimented endlessly. When I first started to learn how to make chocolate decorations, I used to lose my temper because they did not turn out like the ones illustrated in books. Over time, as I perfected a working method, I realised where I was going wrong. I also came to understand the external influences which could affect how my confectionery or ganache topping turned out. The secret is to learn how chocolate reacts to different temperatures and how it may behave when you are handling it. Nowadays I can see at a glance when chocolate is ready to be worked with, just as a baker knows when his bread dough is ready for the oven. Experience is a good teacher.

The tools of the trade

What are the utensils you will need if you want to work with chocolate in your own kitchen at home? Ideally, you should have a double-boiler, a two-tier saucepan with the lower part intended to hold hot water, which can prevent any accidental contact between chocolate and water. If you do not have a double-boiler, a microwave will do. Also essential are the spatulas and scrapers needed to process chocolate during tempering. You should invest in a marble slab as well as a kitchen thermometer. You may find it helpful to buy a series of moulds in order to make chocolate shapes, as well as ramekins and little glass coupes. If you have an electric mixer, it will certainly save you a lot of effort, but if not a hand-held electric whisk will be sufficient. You will then need the appropriate cake tins and, preferably, a fan-assisted oven (but this is by no means essential). Confectionery, mousses and cakes of all descriptions are within everyone's capability. As I always say to beginners who are discovering the world of chocolate for the first time: 'Never give up!'

'Anyone who ever tasted a cup of hot chocolate surrenders a day's travel.'

Johann Wolfgang von Goethe

All about chocolate

Chocolate can be a little difficult to work with. It calls for perseverance and concentration. For the best results, you have to be scrupulous in following precise rules on temperature, cooking times, cooling times and quantities. The main thing is not to give in to discouragement.

Working with chocolate

1 Stainless steel bowls

Indispensable for preparing fillings, toppings, mousses and mixtures; for whipping cream and for whisking egg yolks or egg whites. Stainless steel does not absorb odours and is therefore ideal for a variety of foodstuffs.

1

2

2 Whisks

Essential in patisserie to blend together the various ingredients needed for a mixture. Whisks are particularly useful for whisking egg yolks, egg whites or cream by hand.

3

3 Fine-mesh sieve

It is always best to sift flour, cocoa powder and icing sugar before using them to make fillings and toppings smoother and more homogenous. Use a sheet of baking paper to collect the sifted ingredient.

4 Silicone spatula

This is an extremely useful utensil for scraping up melted or tempered chocolate or indeed any other mixture, from the sides of the bowl in which you have mixed it.

4

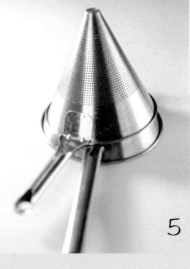

5 Conical sieve (Chinois)

Using this vital utensil will avoid lumps in creamy desserts. It is also useful for sieving liquid or creamy mixtures.

5

7 Knives

For chopping pieces of chocolate to use in fillings and toppings or before tempering.

6 Grater

Essential to grate plain chocolate as decoration or to melt chocolate before tempering it.

7

6

10 Palette knives

These will enable you to spread almost any filling, topping or icing evenly and to level it out, making your creations a feast for the eyes. They are also very useful when tempering chocolate.

8 Hand blender

Ideal for emulsifying fillings, toppings and fruit coulis quickly and effectively.

8

9 Hand-held electric whisks

For the lazier, but also the more demanding cooks. Compared with manual whisks, these whisks enable you to save a great deal of time and energy. They are very useful if you do not have an electric mixer.

9

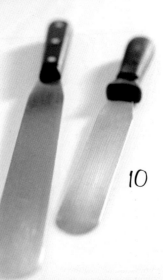

10

Making chocolate shapes

1 Piping bags For piping out choux pastries, meringues and truffles and also useful for piping out bases for cakes and biscuits: these are an essential tool in the creation of chocolate desserts. Try the disposable plastic ones which are more practical and quick to use.

2 Brushes For a more professional finish when spreading out white or chocolate icing on your pastries and also for greasing the base and sides of cake tins with softened butter.

3 Expanding steel multi-cutter Ideal for cutting out decorations from sheets of tempered and crystallised (solidified) chocolate. You can choose the pastry cutter best suited to your design, either smooth or fluted.

4 Multi-shaped biscuit cutters Choose from a whole array of charming cutters, with popular and quirky shapes. These are also useful for creating chocolate decorations to add to your special occasion or birthday cakes.

5 Silicone moulds Ideal for shaping small chocolate cups ready for filling or other confectionery. These moulds are available in a variety of shapes and sizes. The choice is up to you!

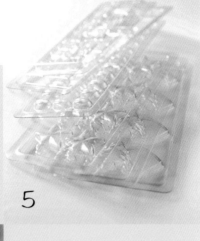

5

6 Flexipan moulds These are for one-portion desserts such as cupcakes. Flexipan is a highly resistant material, which can be used at extremely low temperatures (-40°C/-40°F) and at high ones (280°C/536°F).

6

7 Rolling pin An essential basic utensil, indispensable for rolling out pastry, but also for rolling out some kinds of biscuit dough such as hazelnut biscuit dough (see pages 62–65).

7

8 Heat-resistant plastic moulds Place them on a baking tray when transferring your mixture from the work surface to the oven to avoid spillages.

8

10 Kitchen thermometer Very important in order to check the correct temperature of chocolate and to create syrups, fillings, toppings and meringues.

10

9 Round biscuit cutters Made of either tin or stainless steel, these are invaluable when making biscuits and single-portion treats. In order to protect their cutting edges, they should be stored in a plastic box in between uses.

9

Serving chocolate

1 **Sifter** A practical tool for decorating cakes or semifreddos with a final dusting of best-quality unsweetened or sweetened cocoa powder.

2 **Fluted moulds** These are small moulds made of tin, tinned black steel or aluminium for making tartlets and small cakes; smooth-edged and elongated oval moulds are also available.

3 **Food wrappings and papers** Foil and clingfilm are ideal for storing fillings and toppings, mixtures and cakes prior to serving. Baking paper is essential to prevent biscuits, cakes and tartlets from sticking during baking.

4 **Aluminium moulds** Cooking with aluminium virtually guarantees successful results: this metal heats up quickly and diffuses the heat evenly. It also makes unmoulding very easy. If well polished, it can even be brought to the table.

5 Cake knife In order to serve your cake in the best way, choose a knife that combines stylishness and practicality.

5

7 Large fish slice An indispensable utensil to slide between the side of a cake tin and a cooked cake to loosen it, and also to slide round the inside of a mould to detach a dessert successfully.

6

6 Glass bowl with stand This is ideal for serving desserts eaten with a spoon, and you can also use it for an elegant presentation of small sweet treats arranged in a pyramid, cone or other shape.

7

9 Sauceboat The most elegant way to serve the custard, zabaglione or fruit coulis to accompany your chocolate desserts.

8 Serving tongs Used to serve pastries and tartlets. You will be able to serve your guests so professionally that they will almost have the illusion of being in a patisserie shop.

8

9

10

10 Hot chocolate cups Serve your hot chocolate made with the mixture suggested by our chocolatier (see pages 84–87) in attractive cups.

1

Almond 'flour'

50 g/scant 2 oz icing sugar
50 g/scant 2 oz almonds, skinned and blanched

✔ *It is very easy to make almond 'flour' – an ingredient which is often used in commercial and homemade patisserie. This is sometimes called TPT (from the French* tant pour tant, *meaning the weight of the almonds must be the same as the weight of the icing sugar, no matter what weight of almond 'flour' is specified in the recipe. We demonstrate below and opposite how to make this.*

2

3

4

1 Sift the icing sugar into a food processor, blender or food mixer and add the almonds.

2 Process the almonds and the sugar together until a flour-like consistency is reached.

3–4 Transfer the almond 'flour' mixture to a small bowl and use it as a basic ingredient for your desserts. Almond 'flour' can be stored in an airtight glass container.

Vanilla sugar

✓ *Vanilla is a highly prized ingredient that is irreplaceable in patisserie but is very expensive. Here we show you a few tips and tricks to make the most of vanilla pods and seeds and make this aromatic flavouring last longer.*

1–2–3 Soak five to seven vanilla pods in 500 ml/18 fl oz 95°-proof alcohol or clear spirit (e.g. vodka) and leave to infuse for two weeks. After this time remove the vanilla pods from the spirit, which will now be vanilla-flavoured. Reserve the pods. Lower the alcoholic content of the spirit by mixing it with sugar syrup (see recipe on page 83) – you would need 80–100 ml/3–3 ½ fl oz of sugar syrup to every 500 ml/18 fl oz of alcohol. You can then use the vanilla-flavoured spirit to 'feed' cakes.

4 Dry the reserved vanilla pods and set aside to use in another recipe. When you need to, take a vanilla pod and, using a small sharp knife, open it up lengthways in two sections.

5–6 Scrape out the seeds from inside the pod using a corer or smooth-bladed knife (and discard them or use them in another recipe).

7 To make the vanilla sugar, place cut or uncut vanilla pods in a container of icing sugar and close with a lid. After five days you will have perfect vanilla sugar. You will need three vanilla pods to flavour 500 g/1 lb icing sugar.

1

2

3

4

You can use vanilla seeds to flavour custard or pastry cream:
just add them to the egg and sugar mixture.

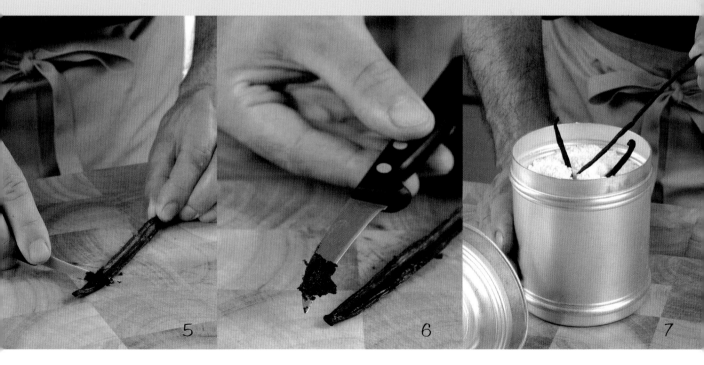

5

6

7

Sponge cake

10 eggs
375 g/13 oz caster sugar
75 g/2½ oz honey
300 g/10 oz plain flour
150 g/5 oz potato flour

1–2 Break the eggs into a bowl and whisk them using a hand-held electric or a balloon whisk. When they are slightly creamy, pour in the sugar and honey in a steady stream, whisking continuously. You should aim to obtain a soft mass of air, eggs and sugar.

3–4 Sift the flours on to greaseproof paper.

5–6 When the egg mixture is white (it should have trebled in volume and you may need a bigger bowl), add the sifted flours in three instalments, stirring with a spoon and mixing.

The pastry chef recommends

✔ *All recipes in this book refer to medium eggs.*

✔ *Combine the eggs with the sugar and honey first, then add the sifted flours. Use acacia honey because it has a more subtle flavour. The addition of the flours helps to stabilise the cake. Without this starch, the cake would collapse in the middle when taken out of the oven.*

✔ *The ideal temperature the eggs should be in order to incorporate air is 34–36°C/93–97°F, so ideally you can work with the eggs at room temperature.*

✔ *Add the sugar and honey when the eggs are whisked. If you add them too soon, the mixture will be too heavy.*

✔ *Using a fan oven ensures better and more even results. If you use an ordinary oven there is always the risk of the bottom of the cake being cooked before the top.*

✔ *You can fill the sponge cake with 500 g/1 lb 1 oz custard (see recipe on page 78), into which you can stir 300 g/10 oz plain chocolate, melted in the microwave.*

1

2

3

For a flavoured sponge cake add vanilla extract,
cinnamon or citrus rind to the mixture.

4

5

6

✔ *To check whether the sponge cake is cooked insert a cocktail stick or small skewer into the centre of the cake. If it comes out dry, the cake is cooked, if some mixture is attached, return the cake to the oven until done.*

✔ *Do not be tempted to open the oven door during cooking. You would cause a drop in pressure, and the cake would be more likely to collapse.*

✔ *To add extra flavour to the basic cake mixture, replace 10% of the flour with almond 'flour' (see recipe on pages 18–19).*

7 Grease two cake tins (one 20 cm/8 in and one 30 cm/12 in diameter) with softened butter, using a brush to help you, and lightly sprinkle the insides with flour.

8 Pour the mixture into each cake tin so that it comes halfway up and smooth the surfaces with a spatula.

9–10–11–12 Bake in a preheated oven at 180°C/ 350°F/gas mark 4 for about 20 minutes. Tap the base of the cake tin on the work surface so that the cake separates more easily from the sides of the tin and turn out. Cut the cake in half horizontally, using a serrated knife. To obtain a neat cut, rotate the cake as you cut it, keeping the knife in the same position.

The thinner the beaters of your whisk, the more air the cake mixture will incorporate.

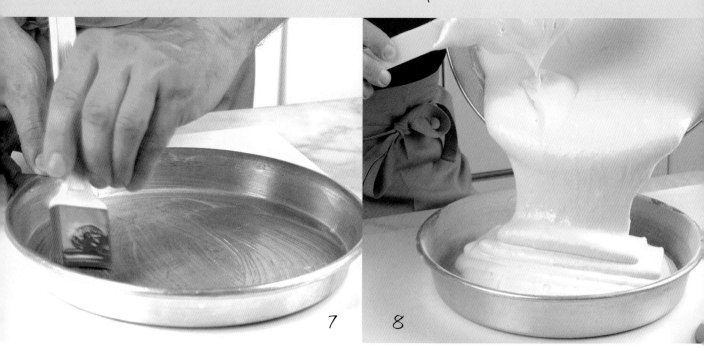

7   8

Viennese sweet pastry

325 g/11 oz cold butter, cut into small cubes
450 g/1 lb plain flour
100 g /3½ oz almond 'flour' (50 g/scant 2 oz icing sugar + 50 g/scant 2 oz ground almonds)
200 g/7 oz icing sugar
2 eggs + 1 egg white, **pinch** of salt

1–2–3 Mix the butter, flour, almond 'flour' and icing sugar in the food processor or mixer at medium speed until your mixture resembles breadcrumbs.

4–5–6 Add the eggs, the egg white and a pinch of salt, mixing for a further 2–3 minutes. Wrap the dough in clingfilm and allow it to rest in the fridge for three hours.

The pastry chef recommends

✔ Gluten comes from the two proteins contained in flour. When these are mixed with water, and with the aid of a mechanical movement, they form the elastic network of gluten.

✔ In this sweet egg pastry gluten's elastic network is barely present: the glutinous chains must be easily broken in order to keep the dough friable. It is therefore important to avoid any direct contact between flour and liquids. The small squares of cold butter are mixed with the flour and sugar: in this way the fat contained in the butter envelops the proteins in the flour and delays the production of gluten until the eggs (the liquid content) are added. Before the addition of the eggs the mixture should resemble fine breadcrumbs. Once the eggs have been added and the dough begins to form, it is time to stop working it. The eggs make the dough more compact and cohesive. By following this sequence when mixing the ingredients together you will have greater control over the dough.

✔ You can work pastry directly with your hands only if you have some dough left over in the fridge and have to 'reactivate' it.

For successful pastry, never handle the
dough directly with your hands.

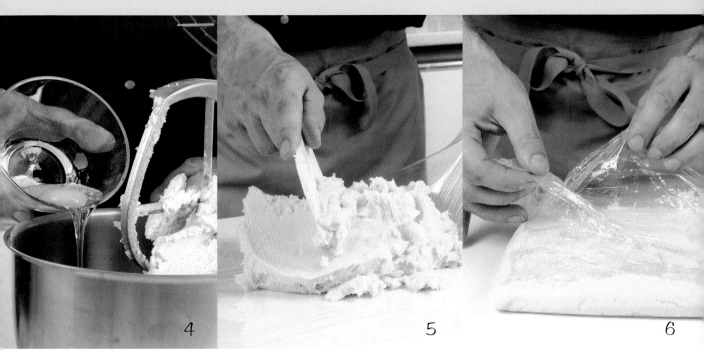

✓ For successful pastry dough, always choose plain flour (made from 'soft' wheat). We recommend '00' flour, which is very finely ground and soft. It is important to handle the mixture as little as possible.

✓ The resting time for pastry is of fundamental importance: it relaxes the elastic network of the gluten that will have formed. It must be chilled in the fridge; the cold will help the fats to re-crystallise and the dough mixture will be firmer and easier to work.

✓ You can use coarse salt instead of beans to bake blind.

7 Once the resting time is over, roll out the pastry with a rolling pin on a lightly floured board or work surface to a thickness of ½ cm/¼ in.

8–9–10 With the aid of the rolling pin, lay the pastry round into two greased and floured 23-cm/9-in flan tins, pressing the edges into the sides of the tin. Cut off any excess pastry. To ensure the pastry does not swell during cooking, place a flan tin of the same size on top of it before you put it in the oven.

11–12 Alternatively, lay a sheet of clingfilm or foil on top of the pastry, and pour dried or baking beans inside. Bake the pastry in a preheated oven at 170°C/325°F/gas mark 3 for 12–15 minutes, take it out of the oven and remove the clingfilm and dried beans.

Using clingfilm in cooking is an excellent idea when cooking at low temperatures and in fan ovens.

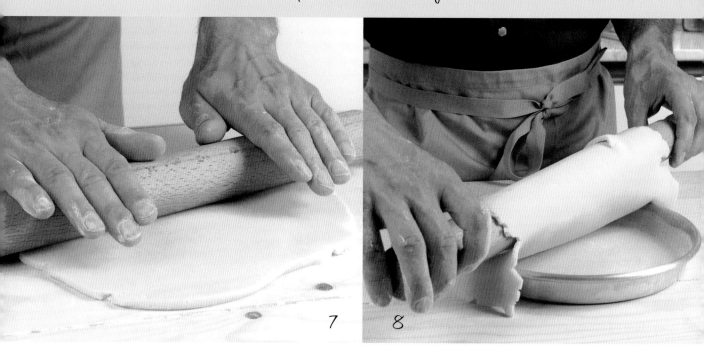

7

8

9

10

11

12

Ganache filling for a pastry case

300 g/10 oz plain chocolate
200 ml/7 fl oz double cream
70 ml/2½ fl oz custard
(see pages 78–79)
40 g/1½ oz butter, softened

1 Cut the chocolate into squares. Heat the cream to boiling point and add to the chocolate squares. Allow the chocolate to melt in the cream without stirring the mixture.

2–3 Once the chocolate has melted, stir, starting from the middle of the bowl, until you have an emulsified mixture.

4–5–6–7 Add the custard and stir. Add the butter and stir until it has completely melted.

8–9 Pour the ganache into a cooled baked 23-cm/9-in pastry case.

The pastry chef recommends

✔ *You can make an icing by using the above ingredients for ganache and adding two gelatine leaves to the boiling cream. This will make the mixture firmer and prevent it from running down the sides of the cake.*

✔ *Alternatively, you can make an icing with 500 ml/18 fl oz double cream, 1 vanilla pod, 180 ml/6fl oz liquid glucose (or sugar syrup, see recipe on page 83), 10 g/scant ½ oz gelatine,*

400 g/14 oz plain chocolate. Once you have mixed these ingredients together, refrigerate the icing until set and use it at a temperature of 38–45°C/100°–113°F.

✔ *When you add the butter, softened at room temperature, into the chocolate and cream mixture it is important to stir slowly and continuously to prevent the ganache from separating.*

5   6

To prevent the ganache from separating, stir in the butter
with a circular movement.

7   8

9

Coconut and chocolate chip cookies

325 g/11 oz cold butter, cut into small cubes
450 g/1 lb plain flour
100 g/3½ oz almond 'flour' (see page 18)
(50 g/scant 2 oz icing sugar
+ 50 g/scant 2 oz ground almonds)
200 g/7 oz icing sugar
2 eggs
1 egg white
pinch of salt
50–100 g/scant 2 oz–3½ oz plain chocolate chips
desiccated coconut, to coat

1–2 Prepare the sweet pastry dough as described on page 26. Stir the plain chocolate chips thoroughly into the Viennese sweet pastry before you leave it to rest.

3 Roll the mixture into one or more sausage shapes on a floured board .

4 Roll the dough in desiccated coconut and chill them in the fridge for about 20 minutes.

5 Cut the chilled dough into 40–50 rounds about 1 cm/½ in thick and lay them on a baking sheet(s) lined with baking paper, leaving sufficient space between them to allow for spreading as they cook.

6 Bake the cookies in a preheated oven at 160–180°C/325–350°F/gas mark 3–4 for 10–12 minutes.

The pastry chef recommends

✔ *This biscuit dough lends itself well to different flavour combinations, such as ground nuts or amaretti biscuits.*

✔ *For a sweeter version of this recipe, replace the plain chocolate chips with milk chocolate chips.*

✔ *These cookies will keep for up to ten days in an airtight container. Store them as soon as they are cool.*

You can replace the plain chocolate chips with finely chopped candied fruit such as lemon or orange peel.

Extra-buttery biscuit dough

425 g/15 oz butter, softened
175 g/6 oz vanilla sugar (see page 20)
2 eggs (reserving about half of one of the egg whites for stages 5–6)
500 g/1 lb 1 oz plain flour
½ tsp salt
35 g/generous 1 oz unsweetened cocoa powder

1 Process the butter in a food mixer for 3–4 minutes at maximum speed or cream it with a hand-held electric whisk. Add the vanilla sugar and process.

2 Add the eggs to the butter and sugar mixture and process.

3–4 Detach the mixing bowl from the mixer and sift in the flour, stirring with a spatula. Add the salt and mix thoroughly.

5–6 Divide the mixture in half and place in separate bowls. Sift the unsweetened cocoa powder into one bowl along with the reserved egg white; stir well.

7 Fill a piping bag, fitted with a fluted nozzle with equal amounts of plain dough and cocoa-flavoured dough, side by side (see photograph 7 overleaf).

8 Pipe small amounts of the two-coloured dough on to a baking sheet lined with baking paper, creating biscuit shapes of your choice and keeping a distance of about 2 cm/¾ in between the biscuits to allow for spreading. This should make about 30–40 biscuits.

9 Bake in a preheated oven at 170–180°C/ 325–350°F/gas mark 3–4 for 10–12 minutes.

The pastry chef recommends

✓ *You can dust the biscuits with icing sugar before serving them.*

✓ *Melt some chocolate in a double-boiler and dip the biscuits halfway into it. Allow to cool and set on baking paper.*

✓ *You can use the same dough for flans and pie cases: using a piping bag, fill the base of the tin with the mixture in a spiral movement, working from the centre of the tin outwards. Once the base of the tin has been covered, pipe an edging all round the circumference of the base to form the side of the pastry case. Fill with jam and bake in a preheated oven at 170°C/325°F/gas mark 3 for about 20 minutes or until light golden brown.*

5   6

Before baking you can sprinkle the cookies with icing sugar, chopped candied or crystallised fruit.

7   8

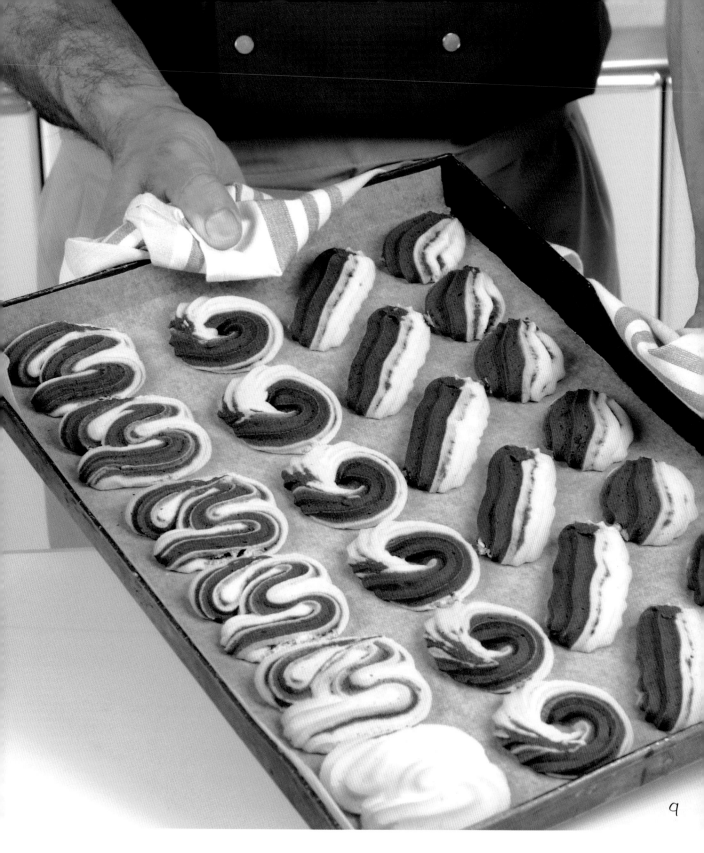

9

Rich chocolate sponge cake

250 g/9 oz butter, at room temperature
250 g/9 oz vanilla sugar (see page 20)
5 eggs
140 g/scant 5 oz potato flour
150 g/5 oz plain flour
30 g/1¼ oz unsweetened cocoa powder
10 g /3 tsp baking powder
200 g/7 oz raisins
200 g/7 oz apples, chopped and soaked in rum
1 unwaxed lemon (grated rind only)

1–2 Cut the butter into small cubes and mix with the vanilla sugar in a bowl or in a food processor. Beat the butter and sugar on medium-high speed in a food processor, or by using a hand-held electric whisk, until the mixture is fluffy.

3 Add about half the eggs and the sifted potato flour to the mixture.

4–5 Sift together the plain flour, cocoa powder and baking powder on to a sheet of baking paper.

6 Add half the plain flour mixture to the butter and sugar mixture and stir well by hand. Add the other half of the flour mixture and the remainder of the eggs and mix well.

7 Add the raisins.

8–9 Flavour the chopped rum-soaked apples with grated lemon rind and add to the cake mixture.

The pastry chef recommends

✔ *If chopped fruit is added, you can replace 50 g/2 oz of the plain flour with strong white bread flour, which will help keep the fruit more evenly distributed.*

✔ *Instead of apples and raisins, you can experiment with other flavour combinations: apple chunks rolled in cinnamon, pear chunks soaked in rum or chopped, stoned cherries.*

✔ *You can make a plain 'white' cake by replacing the cocoa powder with the same amount of plain flour.*

If the fruit is not chopped into small pieces it will be too heavy and sink to the bottom of the cake.

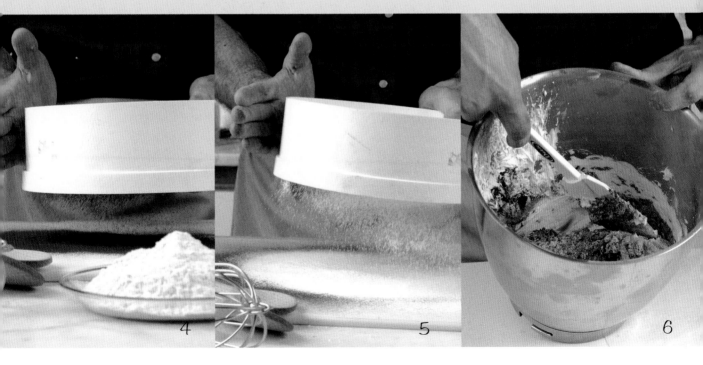

7

10–11 Divide the mixture between two greased and floured 900-g/2-lb loaf tins and bake in a preheated fan oven at 180°C/350°F/gas mark 4 for about 40 minutes. Take the cake out of the tin and leave to cool before serving.

12 This mixture will also make about 30 small cakes: transfer the chocolate and fruit mixture to a piping bag and fill individual-portion rectangular silicone moulds three-quarters full. Bake in a preheated fan oven at 190°C/375°F/gas mark 5 for about 15 minutes.

13–14 Turn out the individual cakes and allow them to cool slightly; dust them with icing sugar. They will keep for four to five days in an airtight container, or you can wrap them in clingfilm and store in the fridge.

8   9

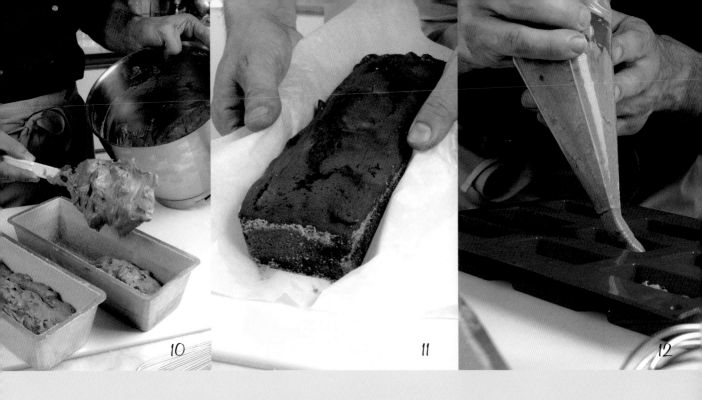

Having greased the tins or moulds, try dusting them with caster sugar instead of flour: this will give the cakes a delicious sugary crust on their sides.

Chocolate profiteroles

1 tsp salt
300 ml/10 fl oz water
300 g/10 oz butter
275 g/scant 10 oz plain flour
25 g/1 oz cocoa powder
8 eggs

1–2–3 Add the salt to the water in a small saucepan. Stir in the butter, melt then bring to the boil. Remove from the heat, add the flour all at once and beat vigorously. The mixture is ready when it leaves the sides of the pan.

4 Transfer the choux pastry to a board to cool, flattening it out with a wooden spoon so that the heat disperses more rapidly.

5 Place the choux pastry in a bowl, sift in the cocoa powder and mix well.

6 Add the eggs gradually to the mixture (two at a time), and stir very well before adding the next batch. The resulting choux paste should be smooth and glossy.

7–8 Put the choux pastry into a piping bag and pipe 30–40 slightly pointed mounds on to a baking sheet lined with baking paper.

9 Bake the profiteroles in a preheated fan oven at 200°C/400°F/gas mark 6 for about 20 minutes. Once you have taken them out of the oven, if you cut one profiterole in half you will see that it should be hollow inside.

10 Fill the profiteroles with chocolate filling: add about 650 g/1 lb 6 oz plain chocolate, (broken into small pieces) to 1 quantity of

The pastry chef recommends

✓ *The choux pastry is ready when the mixture is glossy and holds its shape.*

✓ *If the pastry mixture is not thick enough the profiteroles will not pipe easily into a choux pastry shape; if it is too stiff, it will not rise during cooking and the surface of the profiteroles may crack as they bake.*

✓ *Before baking, sprinkle the profiteroles with caster sugar and, once cooked, split them in half and fill with whipped cream. Close them again and dust the tops with icing sugar.*

Once you have taken them out of the oven, cut the profiteroles in half.
They should be hollow inside.

fairly hot custard (see recipe on page 78) and stir gently until completely melted. Alternatively, add melted chocolate to cold custard and heat the mixture in the microwave or over hot water for about 90 seconds, stirring once or twice.

11–12–13 Make a hole in each profiterole using the nozzle of a piping bag and force in the cool chocolate filling (to speed up the cooling process, you can place the chocolate filling in the fridge prior to using it). When they are full a little bit of filling will protrude from the holes. Finish the profiteroles by dipping them in melted chocolate (plain or white), leave to set and serve.

7

Once you have taken them out of the oven, cut the profiteroles in half. They should be hollow inside.

8

9

Mini madeleines

3 eggs
180 g/6 oz icing sugar
1 unwaxed lemon (grated rind only)
115 ml/4 fl oz full-cream milk
285 g/10 oz plain flour
5 g/2 tsp baking powder
25 g/1 oz unsweetened cocoa powder
30 g/1 oz honey
140 g/5 oz butter, melted

1–2–3 Beat the eggs with the sifted icing sugar and the grated lemon rind. Add the cold milk and mix.

4–5 Gradually add the flour, sifted with the baking powder, to the mixture and stir well to amalgamate all the ingredients.

1

2

To mix the cocoa powder more easily, add it to the milk
before stirring it into the other ingredients.

6 Add the sifted cocoa powder to the mixture.

7 Add the honey and the melted butter (melt this in a microwave or over hot water). Stir until the mixture is smooth and even.

8–9 Leave the mixture to chill and thicken in the fridge for one hour. After this time fill a piping bag with the mixture and pipe it into 40–50 very small silicone madeleine moulds.

10 Bake in a preheated oven at 210°C/400°F/ gas mark 6 until cooked (about 5 minutes). Allow to cool slightly then turn out.

7

8 9

Meringues

8 egg whites
pinch of salt
450g/1 lb icing sugar
50 g/scant 2 oz unsweetened cocoa powder

1–2 Whisk the egg whites with a pinch of salt until stiff with a hand-held electric whisk or in an electric mixer.

3 Gradually add the sifted icing sugar while continuing to whisk the egg whites until the mixture is thick. Icing sugar should always be sifted prior to use to get rid of lumps.

4 Look at the mixture: it should look glossy, firm and compact (the whisking should take 7–8 minutes) and the beaters should leave peaks behind when lifted above the bowl.

5 Divide the mixture in two and add the sifted cocoa powder to one part.

6–7 Place the cocoa-flavoured mixture and the

The pastry chef recommends

✔ *Adding salt to the egg whites stabilises the protein and improves the texture of the meringues. A few drops of lemon juice can be used instead of salt if preferred.*

✔ *Cocoa powder is a very acid substance which tends to denature the proteins contained in the egg. Add it last of all, folding it in delicately with a spoon in order not to lose any volume.*

✔ *When whisking egg whites always use eggs that are at room temperature, rather than cold from the fridge. This makes the whisking faster and more effective.*

✔ *If you have to use cold eggs, the addition of salt or lemon juice becomes even more important: the egg white, which is viscous at the beginning, will 'relax' and will combine with the sugar and cocoa powder more easily.*

plain one in two separate piping bags with a star nozzle and pipe out 25–30 meringues on a baking sheet lined with baking paper.

8 Bake the meringues in a preheated oven at 100°C/212°F/gas mark ¼ for 1½ hours.

✔ *To make successful meringues, you must add the sugar very gradually in a thin stream. In this way you will avoid 'overloading' the mixture and it will absorb the maximum amount of air possible. Start to add the sugar only when the egg whites are stiff and not before.*

5

6

7

Ganache

500 g/1 lb 1 oz good-quality plain chocolate
(64% cocoa solids)
300 ml/10 fl oz double cream
100 g/3½ oz honey
130 g/4½ oz butter, softened
80 ml/3 fl oz whisky

1–2 Heat the chocolate (in small pieces) slowly in the microwave or over hot water until only just melted, then remove from the heat. Warm the cream in a saucepan over a low heat until lukewarm then pour it in a thin stream into the chocolate, stirring gently.

3–4–5–6 Add the honey to the chocolate and cream mixture then add the butter and the whisky. Chill in the fridge for 1 hour.

1

2

3

4

To facilitate the emulsification process mix the
ganache with a hand blender.

5

6

7 During this time take the ganache out of the fridge several times and stir it with a wooden spoon to maintain a uniform consistency.

8–9 Before using the ganache, spread it out in a shallow baking tray to ensure that it is all at the same temperature. This will make enough to ice two 23-cm/9-in cakes.

✓ *Make an icing by adding 20% less chocolate to the mixture.*

✓ *Instead of whisky you could flavour with rum or another spirit or liqueur.*

7

8   9

Truffles

300 ml/10 fl oz double cream
500 g/1 lb 1 oz good-quality plain chocolate
(64% cocoa solids)
100 g/3½ oz honey
130 g/4½ oz butter, softened
80 ml/3 fl oz whisky
unsweetened cocoa powder

1 Make the chocolate ganache following the instructions on pages 56–59. Sift plenty of cocoa powder on to a large, wide plate. Transfer the ganache to a piping bag with a large, plain nozzle and pipe out short lengths, cutting these off from the nozzle opening with a knife repeatedly dipped in iced water and allowing them to fall directly on to the cocoa powder. You should be able to make about 30–40 truffles.

2–3 Using your hands and working as quickly as possible, roll the pieces around in the cocoa, shaping them into little balls; place them on a large plate covered with greaseproof paper and return them to the fridge where they should chill for at least 3 hours until hardened.

4 Once cold, roll the truffles again in cocoa powder if necessary before serving them. Instead of rolling them in cocoa powder, you can roll the truffles in icing sugar, cane sugar, finely chopped nuts, crushed amaretti biscuits or meringues, or in grated milk or plain chocolate.

The pastry chef recommends

✔ *You can vary this recipe by using white chocolate instead of plain, and sugar syrup (see recipe on page 83) instead of the honey. Use the following ingredients: 500 g/1 lb 1 oz white chocolate, 150 ml/5 fl oz double cream, 50 ml/ 2 fl oz sugar syrup, 70 ml/2½ fl oz Grand Marnier, 20 g/scant 1 oz grated orange rind and follow the same method.*

1

2

If the truffles are too soft, increase the quantity of
chocolate by 50–100 g/2–3½ oz.

3

4

Hazelnut and chocolate thins

200 g/7 oz butter, softened
250 g/9 oz icing sugar
35 ml/generous 1 fl oz single cream
3 egg whites
pinch of salt
200 g/7 oz plain flour
30 g/generous 1 oz unsweetened cocoa powder
1 vanilla pod
chopped hazelnuts

1 Cream the butter and sifted icing sugar until fluffy. Add the cream and mix thoroughly.

2 Whisk the egg whites with the salt in a separate bowl until very soft peaks begin to

You can decorate the hazelnut and chocolate thins with chopped nuts of your choice and mixed crystallised fruit if preferred.

7

9

form and gently stir into the butter, sugar and cream mixture.

3–4–5 Sift the flour and the cocoa powder and add to the mixture, followed by the seeds from the vanilla pod (split the pod in half lengthways and, using a smooth-bladed knife, scrape out the seeds). Chill in the fridge for 30 minutes.

6 With two teaspoons dipped in cold water, drop 30–35 teaspoonfuls of the mixture on to a baking sheet lined with baking paper or on a silicone non-stick baking mat and smooth out into rounds with the back of a teaspoon.

7 Alternatively, put the mixture in a piping bag and pipe out flat rounds in a spiral pattern.

8 Decorate the thins with chopped hazelnuts or chopped dried fruit of your choice. Bake in a preheated oven at 200°C/400°F/gas mark 6 for 4–5 minutes 3–4 minutes will be enough if the rounds are small).

9 Take the thins out of the oven and immediately place them on a rolling pin while still very hot: they will sag and acquire their traditional concave shape.

The pastry chef recommends

✔ For crisper thins, add 1 extra egg white to the basic dough, which will result in a more liquid mixture.

✔ For 'white-coloured' thins, omit the cocoa powder and increase the flour quantity by 30 g/1 oz.

8

Plain chocolate mousse

250 g/9 oz plain chocolate, in small squares
200 g/7 oz custard (see recipe on page 78)
400 ml/14 fl oz whipping cream

1–6 Add the chocolate to the very hot custard and stir until its temperature has reduced to 30°C/86°F and the chocolate has melted. Whip the cream and whisk half of it to the mixture, working from the centre towards the outside edges of the bowl until you have a smooth consistency. Add the remaining cream and fold in gently. Chill in the fridge for at least 3 hours before serving. This will make about four–six servings.

1

2

3

4

*For a firmer mousse that holds its shape,
whip the cream until stiff.*

5

6

Milk chocolate mousse

300 g /10 oz milk chocolate
400 ml/14 fl oz whipping cream

1–2 Lightly whip the cream until it just holds its shape. Melt the chocolate over hot water or in a microwave until it reaches a temperature of 50°C/122°F.

3–4 Add one third of the cream to the melted chocolate and, using a hand-held or electric whisk, mix until thoroughly combined. The mixture will begin to solidify slightly. Add half the remaining whipped cream and mix again until the mixture is smooth and glossy.

5–6–7–8 Add the rest of the whipped cream and mix until the mixture is very smooth, working from the centre towards the outside edges and using a spatula to scrape the sides of the bowl if necessary. Chill in the fridge for 1 hour. Serve the mousse in four–six single-portion bowls.

The pastry chef recommends

✔ *Cream that is whipped too stiffly would result in a mousse that is too full of air. This would immediately deflate in your mouth before you had a chance to taste it.*

✔ *When the cream is added, the mixture hardens because chocolate reacts to moisture. It is important to keep stirring in the same direction.*

✔ *You can flavour the mousse with ground spices such as cinnamon, chilli, vanilla. Alternatively, you can add the ground spice of your choice to the unwhipped cream, cover with clingfilm and chill in the fridge overnight. Strain the cream and proceed as above.*

5   6

After it has been chilled in the fridge, the milk chocolate mousse should
have become quite thick as shown in photograph 9 opposite.

7   8

9

Chocolate panna cotta

6 egg yolks
80 g/3 oz caster sugar
1 vanilla pod
250 ml/9 fl oz double cream
250 ml/9 fl oz full-cream milk
150 g/5 oz plain chocolate, melted (see step 6)
butter, for greasing

1–2 Beat the egg yolks with the sugar using a hand-held electric or normal whisk.

3 Split the vanilla pod in half lengthways and, using a smooth-bladed knife, scrape out the seeds. Add these to the egg and sugar mixture and stir well.

1

2

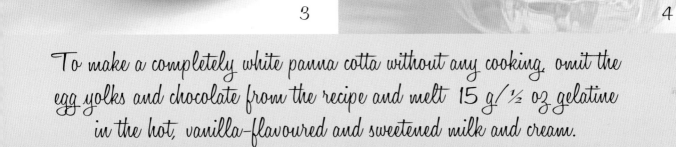

To make a completely white panna cotta without any cooking, omit the egg yolks and chocolate from the recipe and melt 15 g / ½ oz gelatine in the hot, vanilla-flavoured and sweetened milk and cream.

4–5 Gradually add the cream and milk to the egg and sugar mixture, stirring continuously.

6 Take a small amount of this mixture and stir it into the chocolate you have melted in the microwave.

7 Stir the cream and chocolate mixtures together thoroughly until well blended.

8–9 Fill eight–ten greased moulds or ramekins with the mixture.

10 Place the moulds in a deep ovenproof container; add enough hot water to come two thirds of the way up the sides of the moulds. Bake in a preheated oven at 90°C/194°F/gas mark ¼ for about 1 hour. Unmould when cold.

7

8   9

10

Zabaglione

1 vanilla pod
250 ml/9 fl oz Marsala
8 egg yolks
125 g/4½ oz caster sugar

1 Split the vanilla pod in two lengthways and place in a saucepan with the Marsala. Bring to the boil.

2–3 In a separate heatproof bowl or rounded double-boiler whisk the egg yolks and the sugar. Whisk in the warm Marsala and vanilla and cook over hot water, whisking continuously, until a temperature of 82–85°C/180–185°F is reached.

4–5–6 Pour the mixture through a conical sieve into a bowl and immediately place this in iced water to cool before serving.

1   2

3

4

You can serve zabaglione with ice cream, semifreddos made with red berries and all sorts of cake. This mixture will make about six servings

5

6

Custard
(crème anglaise)

250 ml/9 fl oz cream
250 ml/9 fl oz full-cream milk
1 vanilla pod, 5 egg yolks
75 g/scant 3 oz caster sugar

1–2–3 Put the cream, milk and vanilla pod in a saucepan and bring to the boil. In a heatproof bowl or double-boiler, whisk the egg yolks and the sugar.

4–5–6 Remove the vanilla pod. Add the cream and milk mixture to the eggs and sugar and cook over hot water, stirring continuously, until a temperature of 82–85°C/180–185°F is reached. Cool the custard by plunging the bowl into iced water if necessary.

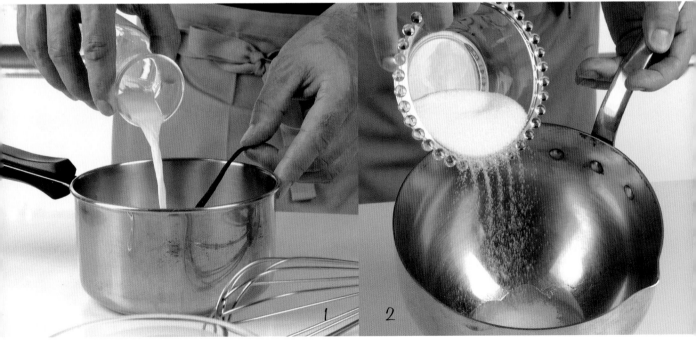

1

2

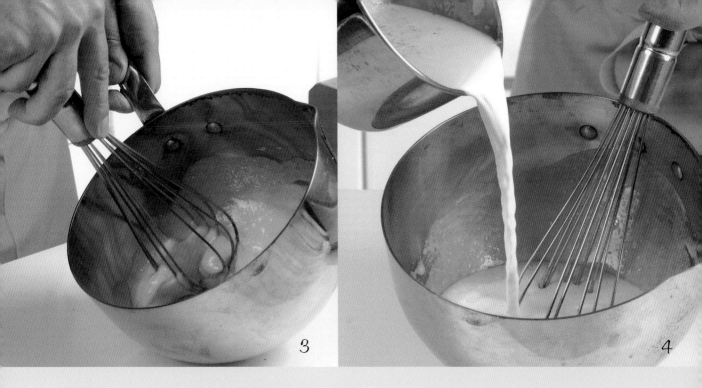

This custard is excellent served with chocolate cake, fruit salad and chocolate puddings. This will make 600–650 ml/1 pt of custard.

Fruit coulis

250 g/9 oz red fruits (one variety only or a mixture)
75 g/2½ oz caster sugar
10 ml/2 tsp Maraschino liqueur
15 ml/1 tbsp lemon juice

1–2–3 Wash the fruit and blend in a food processor or in a bowl using a hand blender. Add the sugar to the fruit and place in a saucepan. Cook, over a low heat, uncovered, for 12–15 minutes, stirring occasionally. The sauce will reduce and thicken. Take off the heat and push the sauce through a sieve to get rid of any little seeds.

4–5 Add the Maraschino liqueur and some or all of the lemon juice to the coulis. Stir well. This will make 200 g/7 oz of coulis.

1

2

3

4

5

Chocolate and hazelnut spread

250 g/9 oz milk chocolate
100 g/3½ oz plain chocolate (70%+ cocoa solids)
250 g/9 oz hazelnut paste (see page 231)
75 ml/3 fl oz sugar syrup
75 ml/3 fl oz sunflower oil

1 Melt the milk and plain chocolate in the microwave or over hot water until it reaches a temperature of 40°C/104°F. Add the hazelnut paste and stir well.

2–3–4–5 Pour in the sugar syrup and stir vigorously: you should end up with a very firm, paste-like mixture. Add the sunflower oil and continue to stir; the final spread should be smooth and semi-fluid, as shown in photograph 5.

6 Transfer the spread to two 250 ml/8fl oz sterilised jars. Do not refrigerate as this will make the paste very thick until it comes to room temperature.

The pastry chef recommends

✔ *Instead of continental plain chocolate pastry cooks tend to use the same amount of cocoa mass. This is obtained from the first toasting and grinding of cocoa beans. It is a kind of very pure chocolate, 99% cocoa solids, a liquefied pulp with no added sugars. Cocoa mass, also known as chocolate liquor, is used in chocolate production.*

To make sugar syrup bring 1 litre/1¾ pts water to the boil with 1.1 kg/2 lb 6 oz granulated sugar.

Homemade drinking chocolate powder

2 vanilla pods
80 g/3 oz best-quality unsweetened cocoa powder
20 g/2 tbsp potato flour
15 g/1½ tbsp cornflour
160 g/5½ oz icing sugar
50 g/scant 2 oz plain chocolate, grated

1 Split the vanilla pods in half lengthways. Using a smooth-bladed knife, scrape out the seeds and mix these with the sifted cocoa powder.

1

2

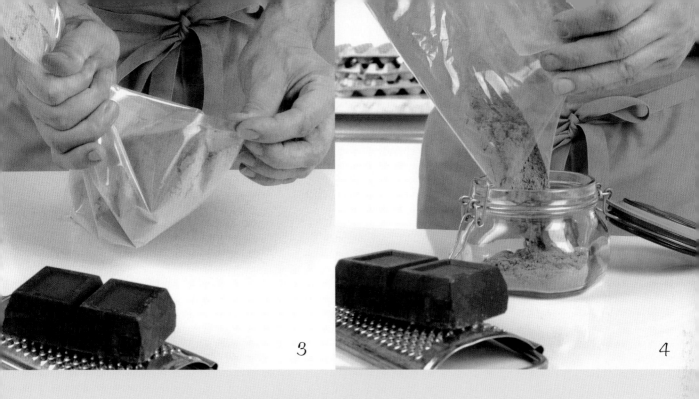

3

4

You can use milk chocolate instead of plain if preferred and flavour the mixture with cinnamon or ground instant coffee.

5

6

2–3–4 Sift the potato flour, cornflour and icing sugar together. Transfer these, together with the grated plain chocolate, to a plastic food bag. Close this and shake well to mix. Transfer the chocolate powder to a 250 g/9 oz sterilised glass jar.

5–6–7 You can prepare the hot chocolate in two different ways: bring a cupful of milk to the boil, put 1 teaspoon of chocolate mixture into the cup and pour the hot milk into it. For a thicker drink, heat in a microwave on a medium setting until the desired consistency is reached.

8–9–10 You can also make the hot chocolate by heating the cold milk and chocolate mixture in a small saucepan over medium to low heat until the desired density is reached.

7

8   9

Decorating with chocolate

You can create innumerable decorations with tempered chocolate using a variety of professional and domestic utensils. Some of the utensils listed in this section can be bought from a DIY shop.

1

2

3

Tempering

Tempering is a special process to treat chocolate before using it to make decorations or confectionery, eliminating the risk of the finished product having a flawed, uneven appearance.

These are the best temperatures for tempering chocolate:

✓ plain chocolate: 31°C/88°F

✓ milk chocolate: 29°C/84°F

✓ white chocolate: 28°C/82°F

If these temperatures are exceeded the chocolate may 'seize' and lose its characteristic shine and consistency and, once crystallised, develop a whitish ' bloom'. The amount of chocolate used in the decorative work we describe is 300 g/10 oz.

1st method
Tempering in a microwave

1 Finely chop the plain chocolate with a knife.

2–3–4 Put it in a bowl in the microwave and heat it on a medium setting, stirring it every 15 seconds until it has completely melted. Use a kitchen thermometer to check the temperature of the chocolate (it must not exceed 33°C/91°C), then use it as directed in the recipe.

4

2nd method
Tempering using the 'seeding' method

1 Grate two thirds of the chocolate and melt the remaining chocolate in the microwave until a temperature of 45–50°C/113–122°F is reached.

2–3 Add the melted chocolate to the grated chocolate and mix together with a spoon until amalgamated.

4–5 The resulting mixture should be at a temperature of 30–32°C/86–90°F.

The pastry chef recommends

✔ *Chocolate tempered using this method will have the liquidity of melted chocolate and the shine and crunch that results from the addition of grated chocolate.*

✔ *If the room temperature where you are working is particularly high it is better to harden the chocolate in the fridge before beginning to grate it.*

✔ *Should the tempered chocolate be too firm, you can make it more fluid by placing it in the microwave for 5 seconds on a medium setting.*

3rd method
Tempering on marble

1 Melt the chocolate in the microwave or over hot water until it reaches a temperature of 45–50°C/113–122°F. Transfer two thirds of the chocolate mixture to a marble slab.

2–3–4–5 Spread out the melted chocolate over the clean marble slab (you can use a steel surface as an alternative to marble) to reduce the temperature to 27°C/81°F.

6–7 Return the chocolate to the bowl, using a scraper, and mix it with the remaining melted chocolate: the resulting mixture should be at a temperature of 30–32°C/86–90°F.

1

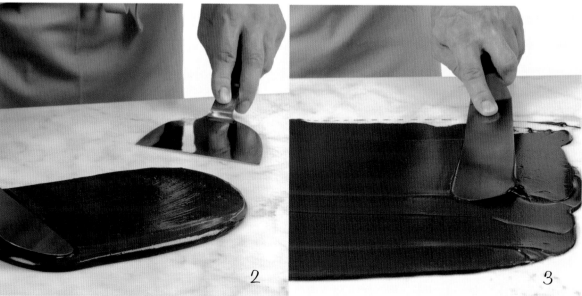

2

3

Decorating with a silicone mould

300 g/10 oz plain chocolate
silicone mould

1–2 Fill a piping bag with tempered chocolate and pipe it into the mould's squares. Tap the bottom of the mould against the work surface to level the chocolate and leave to crystallise.

3–4 Unmould the chocolate squares by turning the mould upside down, quickly and decisively, over a work surface.

1

2

3

4

Textured effects with a plexiglass sheet

300 g/10 oz plain chocolate
plexiglass sheet

1–2–3 Using a palette knife, spread the tempered chocolate over the plexiglass sheet. Leave the resulting decorative textured sheet to crystallise or harden and then carefully remove the sheet of chocolate from the plexiglass.

The pastry chef recommends

✔ Once made, the decoration should dry (the correct technical term is 'crystallise') at room temperature in cold weather and in the fridge in warm weather.

✔ The utensils suggested here are just a starting point. Have fun experimenting with different decorations using various other materials (just make sure they are clean).

Decorative textured effect with an acetate sheet and faux woodgrain comb

300 g/10 oz plain chocolate
300 g/10 oz white chocolate
1 sheet baking paper
faux woodgrain comb

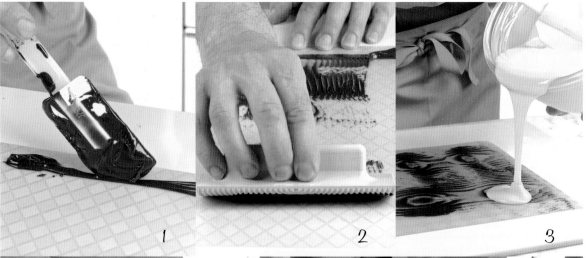

1

2

3

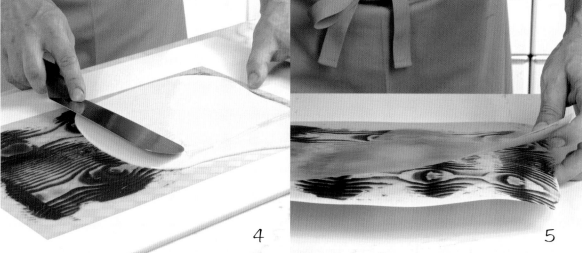

4

5

6

1–2 Spread a thin layer of tempered plain chocolate on the acetate sheet, using the faux woodgrain comb, and allow to set.

3–4 Pour a layer of white chocolate on top of the set plain chocolate, spread it out evenly with a palette knife and allow to set.

5–6 Carefully peel off the acetate sheet from the hardened wood-effect chocolate layer and use the resulting two-tone chocolate to decorate your desserts and cakes.

Decorating with an acetate sheet and draught excluder

300 g/10 oz plain chocolate
300 g/10 oz white chocolate
1 acetate sheet
a length of draught excluder or a palette knife
an expanding steel multi cutter

1 Spread a thin layer of tempered plain chocolate on the acetate sheet, using a length of draught excluder which works particularly well or a palette knife. Allow to set.

2–3 Spread a layer of tempered white chocolate over the set plain chocolate, using a spatula. Allow to set.

4–5–6 Using an expanding steel multi-cutter as shown in the photograph opposite, cut the sheet of two-tone chocolate into squares.

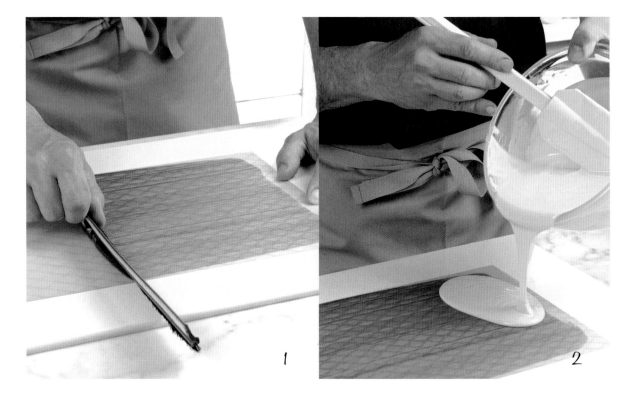

1

2

Decorative effects with bubble wrap

300 g/10 oz plain chocolate
bubble wrap

1–2–3 Pour the tempered chocolate on to the bubble wrap and brush it out so it is ½ cm/¼ in thick all over.

4–5 Once the chocolate has cooled and set, carefully peel off the bubble wrap.

Numbers and letters

300 g/10 oz white chocolate
small biscuit cutters, numerals and letters

1–2 Spread the tempered white chocolate on a sheet of baking paper using a palette knife or brush, to a thickness of 3–4 mm/⅛ –¼ in.

3 Allow the chocolate to set. Use small biscuit cutters to cut out numbers and letters from the sheet of chocolate.

4 Peel off the baking paper and carefully remove the chocolate shapes you have cut out.

Leaf decorations

300 g/10 oz white chocolate
plastic leaves

1–2 Brush a layer of tempered white chocolate all over the surface of each plastic leaf.

3–4 Allow the chocolate to set, then carefully peel off the plastic leaf.

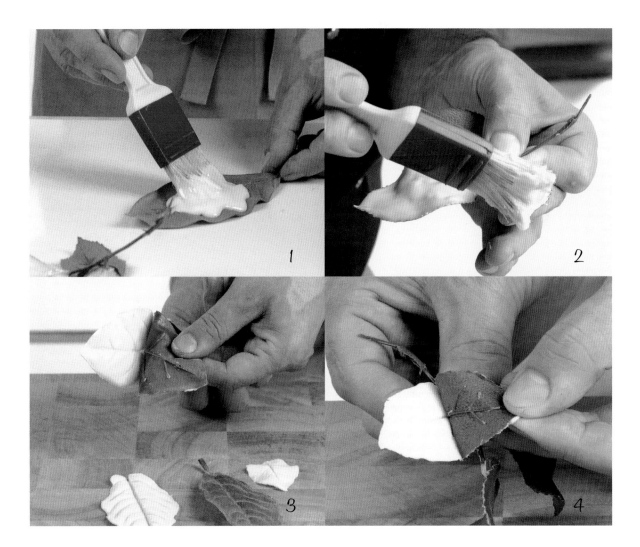

Breakfast-time and beyond

The first meal of the day should give us
a positive energy rush. Muffins, cakes and
biscuits with their tempting aroma of chocolate,
baked sugar and vanilla wake up our bodies
from sleep and put us in a good mood, so
that we start the day with a smile.

Marble cake

*preparation **20 minutes** • cooking time **30 minutes** • easy*

175 g/6 oz butter, softened
130 g/4½ oz caster sugar
1 vanilla pod
3 eggs
225 g/8 oz plain flour
1 tsp baking powder
pinch of salt
50 g/scant 2 oz milk chocolate, melted

Cream the butter with the sugar. Split the vanilla pod in half lengthways and, using a smooth-bladed knife, scrape out the seeds. Add these to the butter and sugar mixture. Add the eggs then the sifted flour, baking powder and a pinch of salt.

Transfer half the mixture to a separate bowl; add the melted milk chocolate to this bowl and stir well. Grease a 23-cm/9-in ring mould with butter and place large spoonfuls of the cake mixture into it, alternating between the chocolate and the plain mixture.

Bake in a preheated oven at 190°C/375°F/gas mark 5 for 30 minutes, then allow the cake to cool in the tin. Turn out the cake and serve it with tea or coffee.

If preferred, the marble cake can be made with plain chocolate instead of milk chocolate. Use the same amount.

Chocolate raisin bread

by Omar Busi

*preparation **40 minutes** • cooking time **15 minutes** • fairly easy*

600 g/1 lb 5 oz plain flour
400 ml/14 fl oz full-cream milk
65 g/generous 2 oz caster sugar
27 g/1 oz butter, softened
10 g/2 tsp salt, 10 g/scant 1 tbsp honey
34 g/1¼ oz (4 sachets) dried yeast
65 g/generous 2 oz unsweetened cocoa powder
200 g/7 oz raisins, soaked in water for 10–15 minutes until plump, then drained and dried

For the topping
3 egg whites
340 g/12 oz icing sugar
7 g/1½ tbsp cocoa powder
10 g/1 tbsp potato flour
125 g/4½ oz almonds, blanched and skinned

Sift the flour in a mound on a pastry board or work surface. Make a well in the centre and pour the milk into it. Stir the milk (by hand or with a spoon to begin with) gradually incorporating all the flour. Add the sugar and the softened butter and work them in. Gradually add the salt, honey, yeast and, finally, the sifted cocoa powder and raisins. Continue kneading until you have a smooth and elastic dough. Place the dough in a large bowl, cover it with clingfilm and leave it to rise at warm room temperature for 30–40 minutes.

Divide the dough into about 15 individual rolls; place these, well spaced, on one or more prepared baking sheet(s) and leave them to rise again, until they have doubled in volume. Make the topping: put the egg white in a bowl and mix in the sifted icing sugar, cocoa powder and potato flour followed by the finely chopped almonds. Chill in the fridge for 2 hours then brush the topping over the rolls. Decorate with flaked almonds.

Bake the rolls in a preheated oven at 200°C/400°F/gas mark 6 for 12–15 minutes. Place a small ovenproof dish of water in the oven: the water will evaporate, helping to keep the rolls moist. You can also make larger loaves, 500 g/1 lb 1 oz each with this recipe; bake them in a preheated oven at 180°C/350°F/gas mark 4 for 20–22 minutes. Insert a thin wooden skewer into the centre of the loaves to check if they are cooked; if it comes out with no mixture attached to it, the loaves are ready.

Chocolate and potato cake

*preparation **20 minutes** • cooking time **80 minutes** • easy*

800 g/1 lb 12 oz floury potatoes
100 g/3½ oz butter
225 g/8 oz caster sugar
1 vanilla pod
100 g/3½ oz ground almonds
1 unwaxed orange (grated rind only)
4 egg yolks
125 g/4½ oz plain chocolate, coarsely grated
3 egg whites
pinch of salt

Put the unpeeled, washed potatoes in cold water and bring to the boil. Cook for about 30 minutes, depending on size, then drain, peel and put through a potato ricer to mash. Transfer the mashed potatoes to a bowl and leave to cool.

Melt the butter over hot water and add it to the mashed potatoes, stirring well. Add the sugar. Split the vanilla pod in half lengthways and, using a smooth-bladed knife, scrape out the seeds. Add these to the potato mixture, together with the ground almonds and the grated orange rind. Mix thoroughly. Add the egg yolks and the coarsely grated chocolate to the mixture.

Whisk the egg whites with a pinch of salt until very stiff and gently fold them in to the mixture. Pour the mixture into a greased 23-cm/9-in spring-release ring mould. Place this in a roasting tin and add sufficient hot water to come two thirds of the way up the sides of the cake tin. Bake in a preheated oven at 180°C/350°F/gas mark 4 for 45 minutes. Leave the cake to cool a little before turning it out on to a serving plate.

When a recipe calls for whisked egg whites, always whisk these just before you need them and add them to the mixture immediately, so they do not start to deflate.

Almond and chocolate tart

*preparation **30 minutes** · cooking time **30 minutes** · fairly easy*

80 g/3 oz butter, softened
400 g/14 oz plain flour
80 g/3 oz caster sugar
1 vanilla pod
1 unwaxed lemon (grated rind only)
a little sweet white wine

For the filling
300 g/10 oz almonds, blanched and skinned
100 g/3½ oz caster sugar
2 eggs
100 g/3½ oz plain chocolate, finely chopped

Make the sweet pastry: combine the butter with the flour using a pastry blender or by rubbing in; stir in the sugar, the seeds from the vanilla pod and the finely grated rind from one lemon. Add just enough white wine to make the pastry less friable and easier to handle. Work briefly by hand until smooth. Chill in the fridge, covered with a cloth, while you make the filling.

Grind the almonds with the sugar in a food processor; transfer to a bowl and mix thoroughly with the eggs and the very finely chopped chocolate.

Line a 23-cm/9-in non-stick flan tin with two thirds of the pastry; fill with the chocolate and almond mixture, spreading it out evenly, and cover with a lattice of strips cut from the remaining pastry. Bake in a preheated oven at 150°C/300°F/gas mark 2 for about 30 minutes. When the tart is cooked, allow to cool before taking it out of the tin. Dust with icing sugar, or drizzle with icing, or serve just as it is, warm or cold.

Traditional sweet short pastry (pâte brisée) is made with flour, butter and cold water, using two parts flour to one part butter. Wrapped in clingfilm, it will keep in the fridge for several days; it can also be frozen.

Moist citrus and milk chocolate cake

*preparation **30 minutes** • cooking time **50 minutes** • fairly easy*

butter, for greasing
150 g/5 oz milk chocolate
1 unwaxed lemon (grated rind only)
1 unwaxed orange (grated rind only)
60 g/generous 2 oz plain flour
1 tsp baking powder
95 g/3½ oz almonds, skinned and blanched
4 egg yolks
125 g/4½ oz caster sugar
15–20 ml/1–1½ tbsp milk, warmed
3 egg whites, **pinch** of salt

For the filling and topping
170 ml/6 fl oz whipping cream
icing sugar

Grease a 23-cm/9-in spring-release cake tin and line the bottom with baking paper. Chop 100 g/3½ oz of the chocolate in the food processor with 1 tablespoon mixed grated citrus rind. Add the sifted flour and baking powder and the almonds; process briefly or until the almonds are finely chopped.

Beat the egg yolks and sugar in a large bowl with a hand-held electric whisk; stir in the almond mixture and the milk. Whisk the egg whites with a pinch of salt until stiff; use a mixing spatula to fold into the cake mixture. Bake in a preheated oven at 180°C/ 350°F/gas mark 4 for 45 minutes. Allow to cool before turning out. Cut the cake in half horizontally.

Melt the remaining chocolate over hot water and spread over the bottom layer of the cake. Spread the stiffly whipped cream on top. Cover with the top layer of the cake. Chill for 20 minutes in the fridge before dusting the surface with sifted icing sugar. If wished, decorate with flakes of milk chocolate.

Lemon pie with white chocolate and blueberries

*preparation **30 minutes** · cooking time **45 minutes** · fairly easy*

350 g/12 oz Viennese sweet pastry
(see recipe on page 26)
3 eggs
125 g/4½ oz caster sugar
2 unwaxed lemons
60 ml/2 fl oz double cream
15 g/1½ tbsp cornflour

For the topping
150 g/5 oz white chocolate
90 ml/3 fl oz whipping cream
100 g/3½ oz blueberries

Roll out the Viennese sweet pastry (see recipe on page 26) on a floured work surface; grease a 20-cm/8-in flan tin liberally with butter, dust with flour and line with the pastry, trimming off any excess around the edges. Prick the base of the pastry case with a fork and chill in the fridge for 20 minutes. Place a sheet of foil inside the pastry case and fill with baking beans to prevent the pastry from rising as it cooks. Place in the oven, preheated to 200°C/400°F/gas mark 6, and bake blind for 10 minutes; remove the beans and foil and leave to cool.

Beat the eggs and sugar together with a hand-held electric whisk; add 1 tablespoon of strained lemon juice and the grated rind of the lemons, the cream and the cornflour. Pour this mixture into the pastry case and bake in the oven, preheated to 180°C/350°F/gas mark 4 for 15 minutes then reduce the oven temperature to 160°C/325°F/gas mark 3 and continue baking for a further 20 minutes.

Allow to cool then remove from the flan tin. To make the topping, melt the white chocolate, mix with the whipped cream and spread over the surface of the pie. Decorate with blueberries and serve.

Cornflour is also used to thicken custards and sauces. Potato flour can be substituted.

Chestnut and chocolate pie

*preparation **30 minutes** · cooking time **95 minutes** · easy*

1 vanilla pod
800 g/1 lb 12 oz sweet chestnuts
300 ml/½ pt milk
250 g/9 oz caster sugar
250 g/9 oz plain chocolate, coarsely chopped
120 g/4 oz mascarpone
350 g/12 oz plain flour
80 g/3 oz butter, softened
1 egg

Split the vanilla pod in half lengthways and, using a smooth-bladed knife, scrape out the seeds and reserve both the pod and the seeds. Cook the chestnuts in boiling water for about 30 minutes, peel and skin them, then purée them in a food mill. Mix the purée in a saucepan with the milk, 100 g/3½ oz of the sugar and the vanilla pod and cook for 10 minutes. Reduce the heat, remove the vanilla pod and add the chocolate; continue cooking until the mixture thickens. Stir in the mascarpone and vanilla seeds; cook for a further 2–3 minutes then remove from the heat. Allow to cool.

Meanwhile, place the sifted flour and remaining sugar in a mixing bowl; add the butter, cut into small pieces. Rub the butter into the flour and sugar with your fingers or use a pastry blender. Add the lightly beaten egg and work into the mixture by hand, adding just enough lukewarm water to make the pastry smooth and homogenous. Use a little more than half the pastry to line a 23-cm/9-in flan tin; fill with the chestnut and chocolate mixture.Use the remaining pastry to make the lid for the pie, pressing the pastry edges together to seal. Use a fork to prick the lid in various places to allow steam to escape. Bake in a preheated oven at 180°C/350°F/gas mark 4 for 45 minutes, or until the edges of the pie are golden brown. Allow to cool before serving.

Alternatively, you could use tinned 700 g/1 lb 8 oz chestnut purée. Mix it in a saucepan with the milk, with 100 g/3½ oz of the sugar, 2 teaspoons vanilla essence and cook for 10 minutes. Or use sweetened chestnut purée and omit the extra sugar and vanilla.

Ricotta and hazelnut praline chocolate pie

*preparation **40 minutes** · cooking time **40 minutes** · easy*

200 g/7 oz butter, softened
400 g/14 oz plain flour, sifted
200 g/7 oz caster sugar
2 eggs
pinch of salt

For the filling
1 vanilla pod
500 ml/18 fl oz full-cream milk
4 egg yolks
125 g/4½ oz caster sugar
50 g/2 oz plain flour
80 g/3 oz praline or gianduia chocolate, grated
100 g/3½ oz very fresh ricotta cheese

Make a rich sweet pastry by rubbing the butter into the flour and sugar and working in the eggs. Place the pastry on a floured work surface and use the 'heel' of your palm to press it away from you, turning the pastry as you work it. Shape into a ball, wrap in clingfilm and chill in the fridge.

Split the vanilla pod in half lengthways and, using a smooth-bladed knife, scrape out the seeds and reserve. Heat the milk with the vanilla pod slowly to scalding point in a saucepan while you beat the egg yolks and sugar in a bowl (using a hand-held electric or balloon whisk). Stir in the flour followed by the hot milk (remove the pod). Pour this custard into a saucepan, add the vanilla seeds and whisk with a balloon whisk over a gentle heat until the custard thickens. Do not allow to boil. Pour into a bowl; add the chocolate and stir with a wooden spoon until it has melted completely. When cool, stir in the ricotta.

Roll out the pastry and use it to line a greased, lightly floured 23-cm/9-in pie tin. Prick the pastry with a fork and add the filling. Cut the remaining pastry into strips and use them to cover the pie, arranged as a lattice. Bake in a preheated oven at 180°C/350°F/gas mark 4 for about 30 minutes. Allow to cool, then chill in the fridge for 1 hour.

If gianduia (hazelnut praline) and almond praline chocolate are unavailable, use good-quality milk chocolate.

Apricot and pine nut cake with chocolate sauce

*Preparation **30 minutes** · cooking time **80 minutes** · easy*

100 g/3½ oz pine nuts
250 g/9 oz butter, softened
250 g/9 oz caster sugar
2 unwaxed oranges (grated rind only)
3 eggs
310 g/11 oz plain flour
3 tsp baking powder
200 g/7 oz dried apricots
250 ml/9 fl oz orange juice

For the chocolate sauce
150 g/5 oz plain chocolate
150 ml/¹/₄ pint double cream

Toast the pine nuts in the oven for a very few minutes, then chop them coarsely. Beat the softened butter with the sugar and the grated rind of the oranges. Continue beating as you add the lightly beaten eggs a little at a time. Use a mixing spatula or wooden spoon to stir in the flour, sifted with the baking powder.

Add the pine nuts, the chopped apricots and the strained orange juice. Transfer to a 23-cm/9-in cake tin, greased and lined with baking paper. Level the surface of the cake mixture and bake in a preheated oven at 175°C/350°F/gas mark 4 for 1 hour 20 minutes.

Remove from the oven and leave to cool for 15 minutes before turning out. Melt the chocolate with the cream and pour a little of this sauce over each serving.

To prevent the apricots sinking to the bottom of the cake as it cooks, toss them in flour and shake in a sieve before adding to the mixture.

Crumbly cocoa cakes

by Omar Busi

*preparation **30 minutes** • cooking time **40 minutes** • easy*

225 g/8 oz butter, chilled
100 g/3½ oz ground almonds
170 g/6 oz icing sugar
1 vanilla pod
2 egg yolks
generous pinch of salt
200 g/7 oz plain flour
scant 2 tsp baking powder
70 g/2½ oz unsweetened cocoa powder
100 g/3½ oz very fine polenta or cornmeal

Cut the cold butter into small pieces. Using a food mixer, hand-held electric whisk or a pastry blender, combine it with the ground almonds, icing sugar and the seeds of the vanilla pod (split the pod in half lengthways and, using a smooth-bladed knife, scrape out the seeds).

Mix these ingredients well in a bowl with the egg yolks and salt. Add the flour, sifted with the baking powder and the cocoa, and the fine polenta. Work the mixture well: it should be rather dry and friable.

Grease a 23-cm/9-in flan tin or 10 individual moulds with butter; spread the mixture out evenly and press down lightly. Bake in a preheated oven at 180°C/350°F/gas mark 4 for 8 minutes, then reduce the temperature to 120°C/250°F/gas mark ½ and bake for a further 30 minutes if baking one large crumbly cake, or for approximately 20 minutes for individual cakes.

You can prepare this mixture by hand; cut the cold butter into very small pieces and work in the ingredients in the same order as briefly as possible to avoid melting the butter. The mixture should look rather crumbly.

Walnut cake with milk chocolate icing

*preparation **30 minutes** · cooking time **40 minutes** · fairly easy*

185 g/6½ oz butter, softened
95 g/3 oz fine cane sugar or caster sugar
2 eggs
185 g/6½ oz plain flour
scant 2 tsp baking powder
pinch of salt
50 ml/2 fl oz milk
100 g/3½ oz walnuts

For the icing
15 g/½ oz butter
120 g/4 oz milk chocolate, coarsely chopped

Beat the butter and sugar with a hand-held electric whisk until pale and fluffy. Gradually whisk in the lightly beaten eggs. Stir in the flour in batches, sifted with the baking powder and salt, alternating with small quantities of milk. Coarsely chop 60 g/generous 2 oz of the walnuts and fold into the mixture. Transfer to a greased and lightly floured 20-cm/8-in cake tin and bake in a preheated oven at 180°C/350°F/gas mark 4 for 35 minutes. Allow to cool a little before turning out.

Make the icing when the cake is cold: melt the butter with the coarsely chopped chocolate over hot water or in the microwave and continue stirring, off the heat, until lukewarm.

Place the cake on a cake rack; pour the warm chocolate mixture over it and spread with a palette knife. Cut the remaining walnuts into thin slices and scatter them over the top of the cake and some cake crumbs from the base of the cake on the sides.

To make this cake even more delicious, make double the quantity of icing and use half of it to fill the cake. Cut the cake horizontally in half and fill with half the chocolate mixture and with whipped cream.

Pancakes with chocolate cinnamon filling

*preparation **30 minutes** · cooking time **25 minutes** · easy*

100 g/3½ oz plain flour
scant 2 tsp baking powder
pinch of salt
1 egg
35 g/generous 1 oz caster sugar
1 vanilla pod
150 ml/5 fl oz milk
20 g/scant 1 oz butter, for cooking the pancakes

For the filling
150 g/5 oz plain chocolate
50 ml/2 fl oz double cream
generous pinch of cinnamon

Sift the flour, baking powder and salt into a mixing bowl. Add the lightly beaten egg, sugar and the seeds from the vanilla pod (split the pod in half lengthways and, using a smooth-bladed knife, scrape out the seeds). Pour in the milk, beating as you do so until the batter is smooth and has no lumps. Leave it to rest in the fridge for 20 minutes.

Chop the chocolate coarsely and melt with the cream and cinnamon in a bowl over hot water, stirring frequently with a wooden spoon. Allow to cool until lukewarm and of a fairly thick, creamy consistency.

Grease a non-stick saucepan with butter and heat slowly. Pour in 1 tablespoon of the batter in the centre, keeping the heat low. Cook for 3 minutes and turn the pancake when the underside is pale golden brown. Cook for a further 2 minutes. Keep warm in the oven. Repeat until all the batter has been used (you should be able to make three–four pancakes). Layer pancakes with some of the chocolate cinnamon filling in between them on each person's heated plate and serve.

Instead of the chocolate cinnamon filling, you can serve chocolate custard (see basic recipe on pages 78–79 and Tip on page 22).

Pistachio cakes with chocolate icing

*preparation **30 minutes** · cooking time **30 minutes** · fairly easy*

4 egg yolks
100 g/3½ oz caster sugar
100 g/3½ oz butter, melted
40 g/1½ oz biscuits, finely crumbled
20 ml/scant 1½ tbsp white rum
1 vanilla pod
40 g/1½ oz fine breadcrumbs
3 egg whites
pinch of salt
20 g/1 generous tbsp runny honey
50 g/ 2 oz pistachios, shelled and peeled

For the icing
250 g/9 oz orange-flavoured dark chocolate

Beat the eggs and sugar together until they are pale and fluffy. Add the very gently melted lukewarm butter and continue whisking. Stir in the finely crumbled biscuits, the rum, the seeds from the vanilla pod (split the pod in half lengthways and, using a smooth-bladed knife, scrape out the seeds) and the breadcrumbs.

Whisk the egg whites with a pinch of salt until stiff and fold into the cake mixture using a rubber mixing spatula or a wooden spoon. Add the honey and the finely chopped pistachios. Grease and lightly flour six dariole moulds or a bun tray and fill each mould two-thirds full; bake in a preheated oven at 180°C/350°F/gas mark 4 for about 20–25 minutes (test with a cocktail stick). Allow to cool before turning out.

Temper the chocolate for the icing following any one of the methods described on pages 90–95. Place the cakes on a cake rack and coat or decorate the tops with the chocolate. Allow the chocolate to set before serving.

With a few exceptions, cakes should always be completely cold before they are iced or decorated.

Little milk-chocolate custards

*Preparation **30 minutes** · cooking time **30 minutes** · easy*

375 ml/13 fl oz milk
½ vanilla pod
70 g/2½ oz milk chocolate, grated
150 ml/5 fl oz double cream
3 egg yolks
100 g/3½ oz caster sugar

For the topping
70 g/2½ oz unsweetened cocoa powder
200 ml/7 fl oz whipping cream
30 g/1 oz plain chocolate

Heat the milk in a heatproof mixing bowl over gently simmering water with the vanilla pod, split lengthways in half. Turn off the heat and leave to stand for 20 minutes. Remove the vanilla pod and add the chocolate and the cream. Leave to melt.

Beat the egg yolks and sugar with a hand-held electric or balloon whisk until pale and fluffy; stir gently but thoroughly into the milk mixture. Place six ramekin dishes in a roasting pan or similar ovenproof dish and fill them three-quarters full with the custard mixture. Pour sufficient hot water into the roasting pan to come at least halfway up the side of the dishes. Carefully transfer to a preheated oven and bake at 170°C/350°F/gas mark 4 for 30 minutes, or until set.

Remove the dishes from the bain-marie and allow to cool before sprinkling the surface of the custards with sifted cocoa. Top with a swirl of whipped cream and finish with some chocolate flakes.

You can flavour the milk with a cinnamon stick instead of the vanilla pod if preferred.

Chocolate hazelnut cakes with white chocolate icing

*preparation **20 minutes** · cooking time **30 minutes** · easy*

200 g/7 oz hazelnuts, blanched and skinned
180 g/6 oz butter
5 egg whites
155 g/5 oz plain flour
30 g/1 oz unsweetened cocoa powder
250 g/9 oz icing sugar

For the icing
80 g/3 oz white chocolate, coarsely chopped

Chop the hazelnuts finely in a food processor. Melt the butter over a medium heat in a small saucepan; watch carefully as it cooks for four minutes, removing it as soon as it starts to colour. Whisk the egg whites stiffly.

Sift the flour, cocoa powder and icing sugar into a mixing bowl; add the chopped hazelnuts and fold in the stiffly beaten egg white and, lastly, the melted butter. Mix gently but thoroughly and spoon into a 12-portion non-stick bun tray (the bendable, lattice type is easy to use), half-filling each mould. Bake in a preheated oven at 200°C/400°F/gas mark 6 for 20–25 minutes. Insert a cocktail stick in the centre of one of the cakes, to check if they are cooked; if it comes out with no mixture attached to it, the cakes are ready.

Heat the chocolate in a bowl over hot water; as soon as it starts to melt, remove from the heat. Stir as it cools and, when smooth and starting to thicken, drizzle the melted chocolate over the cakes or pipe a lattice decoration using a piping bag and fine nozzle.

You can make your own piping bag by cutting out a triangle of greaseproof paper, overlapping the edges to form a cone, folding over the top and snipping off the pointed end; fill with the melted chocolate and pipe.

Crumbly biscuits with milk chocolate

*preparation **30 minutes** • cooking time **15 minutes** • easy*

125 g/4½ oz butter, softened
125 g/4½ oz caster sugar
2 egg yolks
1 vanilla pod
155 g/5 oz plain flour
110 g/4 oz very fine polenta or cornmeal
pinch of bicarbonate of soda
60 g/2 oz milk chocolate chips
icing sugar, to dust (optional)

Beat the butter with the sugar until pale and fluffy; stir in the egg yolks and the vanilla pod seeds (split the pod in half lengthways and, using a smooth-bladed knife, scrape out the seeds). Gradually incorporate the sifted flour and the fine polenta, followed by a generous pinch of bicarbonate of soda.

Work the mixture briefly by hand, just enough to make it hold together. Roll or press out on a sheet of foil, cover with clingfilm and chill for at least 1 hour in the fridge.

Divide the mixture into four equal portions; add one quarter of the chocolate chips to each portion, then combine all the portions together and roll out with a rolling pin on a lightly floured work surface.

Cut out the dough with your chosen shape of pastry cutter into 30–35 biscuits and place on top of a baking tray lined with baking paper. Bake in a preheated oven at 160°C/325°F/gas mark 3 for about 15 minutes. When cold, sprinkle with icing sugar if wished and serve.

You can vary this recipe by adding your choice of extra ingredients, such as 4–5 tablespoons of sultanas or 3–4 tablespoons of desiccated coconut.

Chocolate cookies

100 g/3½ oz plain chocolate
50 g/2 oz butter
55 g/generous 2 oz sugar
1 egg
1 vanilla pod
110 g/4 oz plain flour
15 g/½ oz unsweetened cocoa powder
generous pinch each of baking powder
and salt
35 g/1–1½ oz icing sugar

Break the chocolate into small pieces and melt it in a bowl over hot water with the butter, stirring well. Remove from the heat; add the sugar and continue stirring for a few minutes. Stir in the egg and the seeds from the vanilla pod (split the pod in half lengthways and, using a smooth-bladed knife, scrape out the seeds). Sift the flour with the cocoa powder, baking powder and salt and gradually add this to the chocolate mixture, stirring well.

Grease one or more baking sheets and dust with flour. Take a tablespoonful of the mixture at a time, shape it into a ball and roll in the sifted icing sugar, shaking off any excess. Press all these gently on to the baking sheet, well spaced apart (you should be able to make 25–30 cookies).

Bake the cookies in a preheated oven at 160°C/325°F/gas mark 3 for 20 minutes, removing them when they are firm to the touch on their outsides. Allow to cool for a few minutes before using a spatula to loosen them from the baking sheet. Cool completely on a cake rack before serving.

If you have a small ice cream scoop, you can use this to shape the mixture instead of shaping by hand.

White chocolate sponge cakes

*preparation **30 minutes** · cooking time **25 minutes** · easy*

125 g/4½ oz butter, softened
180 g/6 oz caster sugar
2 eggs
1 vanilla pod
250 g/9 oz plain flour
3 tsp baking powder
110 ml/scant 4 fl oz single cream
250 g/9 oz white chocolate, coarsely grated

For the topping
20 g/2 tbsp icing sugar
100 g/3½ oz soft cream cheese
50 g/2 oz white chocolate
30ml/2 tbsp single cream

Cream the butter and caster sugar with a hand-held electric whisk until pale and fluffy. Beat in the eggs, followed by the seeds from the vanilla pod (split the pod in half lengthways and, using a smooth-bladed knife, scrape out the seeds). Use a mixing spatula to stir in the sifted flour and baking powder in batches, alternating with the cream. Stir in the grated chocolate.

Spoon the mixture into 12–15 greased dariole or popover moulds (or deep cupcake cases); these should be half-full. Bake in a preheated oven at 170°C/350°F/gas mark 4 for 15–20 minutes. When cold, turn out of the moulds.

Mix the icing sugar thoroughly with the cream cheese. Melt the chocolate with the cream over hot water and stir into the sweetened cream cheese. Cover the tops of the cakes with this topping, smoothing with the back of the spoon. Chill in the fridge for 10 minutes before serving.

For a more chocolatey taste, you can use plain or milk chocolate instead of white chocolate for the topping.

Chequerboard biscuits

*preparation **20 minutes** · cooking time **10 minutes** · easy*

370 g/13 oz plain flour
250 g/9 oz caster sugar
200 g/7 oz butter, softened
3 eggs, lightly beaten
pinch of salt
1 vanilla pod
30 g/1 oz milk chocolate

Sift the flour into a mixing bowl, add the sugar, the butter (cut into small pieces), two of the beaten eggs, a pinch of salt and the seeds from the vanilla pod (split the pod in half lengthways and, using a smooth-bladed knife, scrape out the seeds). Work all these ingredients together until the mixture is smooth and homogenous.

Split the mixture in two. Melt the milk chocolate over hot water or in the microwave and work it evenly into one half of the mixture. Wrap both portions in clingfilm and chill in the fridge for 30 minutes.

Roll out the light and dark biscuit mixtures with a rolling pin into two sheets, each approximately 1 cm/⅜ in thick. Grease and line a 28- x 18-cm/11- x 7-in cake tin. Cut the dough sheets into strips of an even width (about 1 cm/⅜ in wide) and arrange these to fit snugly in the tin, alternating the colours. Brush the surface of this first layer liberally with two thirds of the remaining lightly beaten egg and place another layer of strips on top, dark strips on top of light ones and vice versa, pressing down very gently. Brush the surface of the top layer with the last of the remaining beaten egg.

Chill for 20 minutes in the fridge then slice vertically to produce chequered rectangles of biscuit dough. Place carefully on a greased baking sheet and bake in a preheated oven at 180°C/350°F/gas mark 4 for about 10 minutes. Allow to cool completely before serving.

These biscuits go very well with coffee or tea and they are fun for children, served with hot chocolate.

Coffee break

It's a good idea to have a little
mid-morning or mid-afternoon treat with tea,
coffee, chocolate or milk. However small and
insubstantial, these light, sweet snacks
are something to look forward to: they
brighten up the day and are easy to take
to work or to school.

Milk chocolate and praline crunchies

by Omar Busi

*preparation **30 minutes** · cooking time **10 minutes** · easy*

300 g/10 oz granulated or caster sugar
100 ml/3½ fl oz water
800 g/1 lb 12 oz flaked almonds
750 g/1 lb 10 oz milk chocolate
100 g/3½ oz Rice Krispies

Heat the sugar and water together in a small saucepan and boil; set this syrup aside.

Spread the almonds out in a cake tin, add the sugar syrup and mix well. Place in the oven, preheated to 190°C/375°F/gas mark 5 and cook, stirring and turning very frequently, until the mixture has caramelised. Allow to start cooling. Temper the milk chocolate following one of the methods described on pages 90–95.

When the caramelised almonds have cooled to 30°C/86°F, mix them quickly with the Rice Krispies and the tempered chocolate.

Stir well. Using two spoons, arrange the mixture in 40–50 small heaps on a baking tray covered with baking paper or, alternatively, transfer the mixture into small, round silicone moulds. Allow to cool and set. If moulds are used, unmould the crunchies when cold.

To speed up the cooling of the caramelised almonds, you can transfer them to a cold dish, lined with greaseproof paper.

Melting chocolate macaroons

*preparation **30 minutes** · cooking time **25 minutes** · easy*

380 g/13 oz icing sugar
50 g/2 oz unsweetened cocoa powder
125 g/4 oz ground almonds
5 egg whites
pinch of salt

For the ganache filling
250 g/9 oz plain chocolate
150 ml/5 fl oz double cream
20 g/scant 1 oz butter

Sift the icing sugar with the cocoa into a mixing bowl; add the ground almonds and stir well. Whisk the egg whites with a pinch of salt until stiff and fold gently but thoroughly into the almond mixture with a mixing spatula.

Cover one or more baking trays with baking paper. Using a piping bag fitted with a wide nozzle, pipe an even number of similarly sized small mounds of the mixture on to the paper (you should be able to make 20–30 macaroons). Place in a preheated oven at 200°C/400°F/gas mark 6 for about 15 minutes; remove from the oven and allow to cool.

Make the ganache filling: break the chocolate into small pieces and place in a bowl. Heat the cream to boiling point and pour over the chocolate. Add the butter immediately and stir well until the ganache is smooth and homogenous.

Pipe a little ganache on to the flat side of a macaroon and press the flat side of another macaroon gently on to it. Assemble the rest of the macaroons in the same way. Chill until shortly before serving.

There are many different recipes for these macaroons but their appearance and consistency is always the same: crisp and crunchy on the outside, melting and chewy inside.

Speckled chocolate cookies

*preparation **20 minutes** · cooking time **15 minutes** · easy*

140 g/5 oz milk chocolate,
broken into small pieces
100 g/3½ oz butter, softened
80 g/3 oz caster sugar
80 g/3 oz unrefined cane sugar
pinch of salt
1 egg
150 g/5 oz plain flour
1 tsp baking powder
1 vanilla pod
50 g/2 oz pine nuts, chopped
100 g/3½ oz white chocolate,
coarsely chopped

Melt the milk chocolate over hot water or in the microwave. Beat the butter in a mixing bowl with the caster and cane sugar and the salt until very fluffy and creamy. Beat in the egg.

Add the melted, warm (not hot) milk chocolate gradually to the mixture. Combine thoroughly and then add the sifted flour and baking powder and the vanilla seeds (split the pod in half lengthways and, using a smooth-bladed knife, scrape out the seeds), stirring with a wooden spoon. Add the chopped pine nuts and the chopped white chocolate. Mix briefly.

Cover a baking tray with baking paper; shape 20–25 spoonfuls of the mixture into balls and place them on the baking tray, pressing and flattening them. Bake in a preheated oven at 180°C/350°F/gas mark 4 for 13 minutes; remove from the oven and allow to cool. If they are not to be served at once, store the cookies in an airtight biscuit tin.

Leave 3 cm/just over 1 in space between the flattened balls of cookie dough or they may become attached to one another as they rise and spread during cooking.

Muesli, chocolate and ginger biscuits

*preparation **15 minutes** · cooking time **15 minutes** · easy*

130 g/4½ oz muesli
70 g/2½ oz plain flour
50 ml/2 fl oz rice malt syrup
35 ml/generous 1½ fl oz sesame oil
milk

For the topping
70 g/2½ oz plain chocolate

To decorate
17 ml/1 tbsp rice malt syrup
1½ tbsp water
thin slivers of peeled fresh ginger

Place the muesli in a food processor and process until it is reduced to a very fine, floury consistency. Mix in a bowl with the plain flour, rice malt syrup, sesame oil and just enough milk to make a firm, homogenous biscuit dough.

Wrap the biscuit mixture in clingfilm and allow to rest in a cool place for 20 minutes, then roll or press out into a fairly thick sheet and cut out into 25–30 discs with a pastry cutter. Bake in a preheated oven at 180°C/350°F/gas mark 4 for 15 minutes. Allow to cool.

Make candied ginger slivers: heat the rice malt syrup and water; mix the ginger slivers with this light syrup then drain them before placing them on a baking tray covered with baking paper. Put them in the oven, on the lowest possible setting, and leave them to dry out for 1½ hours.

Melt the chocolate over hot water and use it to cover about half of each biscuit. Place a sliver of ginger on the chocolate before it sets. Serve when the chocolate has hardened.

Porridge oats can be processed to a fine, floury consistency if you have no muesli. You can use slivers of bought crystallised ginger instead of fresh to save time.

Mini madeleines

by Omar Busi

*preparation **30 minutes** · cooking time **5 minutes** · easy*

3 eggs
180 g/6 oz icing sugar, sifted
1 unwaxed lemon (grated rind only)
115 ml/4 fl oz full-cream milk
285 g/scant 10 oz plain flour
2 tsp baking powder
25 g/1 oz unsweetened cocoa powder
30 g/1½ tbsp runny honey
140 g/scant 5 oz butter, melted

Beat the eggs and sifted icing sugar together with the grated lemon rind. Add the milk and mix well.

Add the sifted flour, baking powder and cocoa powder gradually, mixing thoroughly.

Stir in the honey and butter (melted over hot water or in the microwave). The mixture should be thick but smooth and homogenous.

Chill for 1 hour in the fridge. Use a piping bag and plain nozzle to fill 40–50 very small, greased and floured tin or silicone madeleine cake moulds (which come in trays).

Bake in a preheated oven at 210°C/420°F/gas mark 7 for about 5 minutes. Allow to cool slightly before turning the cakes out of their moulds.

Some cooks prefer to mix the cocoa powder with the milk and add this before the flour and baking powder. If baked in standard-sized madeleine moulds allow 10 minutes' cooking time.

Little chocolate cupcakes

*preparation **15 minutes** · cooking time **20 minutes** · easy*

125 g/4½ oz butter, softened
90 g/3 oz caster sugar
30 g/1 oz cane sugar
2 eggs
200 g/7 oz plain flour
5 tsp baking powder
15 g/½ oz cocoa powder
pinch of salt
150 ml/5 fl oz milk
1 vanilla pod
60 g/generous 2 oz plain chocolate chips

Beat the butter in a mixing bowl, gradually adding the caster sugar and cane sugar. Beat the eggs lightly and gradually stir them into the butter and sugar mixture.

Sift the flour, baking powder, cocoa and a pinch of salt and add in batches to the mixture, alternating with the milk and stirring after each addition. Stir in the seeds from the vanilla pod (split the pod in half lengthways and, using a smooth-bladed knife, scrape out the seeds) and the chocolate chips.

Spoon into 12–15 cupcake paper cases (or 20–30 mini cupcake cases); these should be two-thirds full. Bake in a preheated oven at 190°C/375°F/gas mark 5 for about 20 minutes. Allow to cool before serving.

If the paper cupcake cases are a little flimsy, use two for each cake (one inside the other) or foil cases to prevent the cupcakes being misshapen.

Orange and chocolate cupcakes

*preparation **20 minutes** · cooking time **55 minutes** · easy*

100 g/3½ oz caster sugar
3 eggs
150 g/5 oz ground almonds
30–40 ml/1–1½ fl oz Amaretto liqueur
150 g/5 oz plain chocolate
50 g/2 oz butter
2 tsp baking powder
1 vanilla pod
10 g/1 tbsp potato flour or cornflour
5 drops essential oil of orange

To decorate
icing sugar

Beat the sugar and eggs in a mixing bowl until they are pale and fluffy. Stir in the ground almonds and the Amaretto liqueur.

Melt the chocolate with the butter over hot water, stir well; pour slowly into the sugar and egg mixture while mixing thoroughly. Stir in the baking powder and the seeds from the vanilla pod (split the pod in half lengthways and, using a smooth-bladed knife, scrape out the seeds), followed by the potato flour (or cornflour) and the orange oil.

Mix until smooth and homogenous. Transfer to 10–12 greased and floured dariole moulds (filling them only two-thirds full) or a deep bun tray and bake in a preheated oven at 180°C/350F°/gas mark 4 for 50 minutes. Remove from the oven and dust with sifted icing sugar when cold.

Essential oil of bitter oranges is used in cocktails while sweet orange oil and orange flower water are ideal for cakes, ice creams and non-alcoholic drinks.

Yellow-fruit and cornflake chocolate bars

by Omar Busi

*preparation **30 minutes** · easy*

600 g/1 lb 5 oz plain or white chocolate
100 g/3½ oz cornflakes
100 g/3½ oz dried apricots
100 g/3½ oz candied orange peel
70 g/2½ oz white chocolate
60 g/2 oz cocoa butter

Temper the plain or white chocolate following one of the methods shown on pages 90–95, then spread it out in a thin layer (approximately 3 mm/⅛ in thick) in a 60- x 40-cm/24- x 16-in flexipan (it should be internally divided into lots of recatngles). Leave undisturbed to start setting while you prepare the topping.

Mix the cornflakes with the chopped dried apricots and orange peel in a mixing bowl. Melt the white chocolate and cocoa butter together over hot water or in the microwave and pour all over the cornflake mixture. Stir well.

Spoon an even layer of this cornflake and fruit mixture on to the partially set tempered chocolate. Chill in the fridge to harden.

Cocoa butter can be ordered online. If you cannot buy it, use 130 g/4½ oz white chocolate instead of 70 g/2½ oz.

Red-fruit and cornflake chocolate bars

by Omar Busi

*preparation **30 minutes** · easy*

600 g/1 lb 5 oz white chocolate
100 g/3½ oz cornflakes
100 g/3½ oz dried strawberries
100 g/3½ oz dried raspberries (and/or dried redcurrants)
70 g/2½ oz white chocolate
60 g/2 oz cocoa butter

Temper the chocolate following one of the methods illustrated on pages 90–95, then spread it out in a thin layer (approximately 3 mm/⅛ in thick) in a 60- x 40-cm/24- x 16-in flexipan (it should be internally divided into lots of recatngles). Leave undisturbed to start setting while you prepare the topping.

Mix the cornflakes with the dried strawberries, cut into small pieces, and the other dried red fruits in a mixing bowl. Melt the white chocolate and cocoa butter together over hot water or in the microwave and sprinkle all over the cornflake mixture. Stir quickly and thoroughly.

Cover the partially set tempered chocolate with an even layer of this cornflake and fruit mixture, pressing down gently with the back of a spoon. Chill in the fridge to harden.

You can vary this recipe by using different cereals and dried fruits.

Purple-fruit and cornflake milk-chocolate bars

by Omar Busi

*preparation **30 minutes** • easy*

600 g/1 lb 5 oz milk chocolate
100 g/3½ oz cornflakes
100 g/3½ oz ready-to-eat prunes
100 g/3½ oz dried blackberries or
dried blueberries
70 g/2½ oz white chocolate
60 g/2 oz cocoa butter

Temper the chocolate following one of the methods illustrated on pages 90–95, then spread it out in a thin layer (approximately 3 mm/⅛ in thick) in a 60- x 40-cm/24- x 16-in flexipan (it should be internally divided into lots of recatngles). Leave undisturbed to start setting while you prepare the topping.

Mix the cornflakes with the prunes (cut into small pieces) and the other dried fruits in a mixing bowl. Melt the white chocolate and cocoa butter together over hot water or in the microwave and sprinkle all over the cornflake mixture. Stir quickly and thoroughly.

Cover the partially set tempered chocolate with an even layer of this cornflake and fruit mixture, pressing down gently with the back of a spoon. Chill in the fridge to harden.

You can experiment with all sorts of combinations of chocolate, cereal and dried fruits. Crushed almond brittle (also called praline and nougatine) is a delicious addition.

Ladies' kisses

*preparation **30 minutes** · cooking time **30 minutes** · easy*

125 g/4½ oz hazelnuts, blanched
and skinned
125 g/4½ oz candied orange peel
125 g/4½ oz flour
125 g/4½ oz sugar
125 g/4½ oz butter, chilled and cut
into small pieces
a little milk
125 g/4½ oz plain chocolate

Chop the hazelnuts very finely; chop the candied orange peel finely.

Mix the sifted flour with the hazelnuts, sugar, orange peel and the butter pieces. Combine all these ingredients by hand, adding a little milk if the mixture is too stiff and/or at all crumbly. Transfer to a piping bag with a plain nozzle and pipe an even number of little mounds of mixture the size of a walnut on to a greased baking sheet, spaced well apart (you should be able to make 20–25 cookies). Bake in a preheated oven at 160°C/325°F/gas mark 3 for about 30 minutes. Remove from the oven and allow to cool.

Melt the chocolate over hot water. When the cookies are cold, spread a little melted chocolate on the flat side of one half and immediately press the flat side of another cookie gently against it. Fill and sandwich the remaining cookies together. Serve when the chocolate has cooled and set.

You can also use apricot jam instead of chocolate for the filling.

Mini chocolate diplomat cakes

*preparation **20 minutes** · cooking time **5 minutes** · fairly easy*

220 g/8 oz milk chocolate
180 g/6 oz plain chocolate
2 eggs + 2 extra yolks
240 g/9 oz caster sugar
15 g/½ oz leaf gelatine or substitute
300 ml/10 fl oz whipping cream
500 g/1 lb–1 lb 4 oz rectangular bought
or home-made sponge cake
100 ml/3½ fl oz rum

To decorate
icing sugar
milk chocolate

Melt the milk chocolate and the plain chocolate in separate mixing bowls over hot water. Use a hand-held electric or a balloon whisk to whisk the eggs and extra yolks with the sugar until pale and greatly increased in volume in a separate bowl.

Soak the leaf gelatine in cold water, blot dry and place half in each of the bowls containing the melted chocolate. Allow to dissolve slowly and completely, stirring now and then. Remove from the heat. Combine half of the whisked egg and sugar mixture with each bowl of melted chocolate, stirring gently. Fold in half the whipped cream into each bowl.

Cut the sponge cake horizontally into three rectangular slices and sprinkle these with the rum diluted with a little cold water. Spread the milk chocolate mixture on top of the first layer, cover with the second layer and spread this with the plain chocolate mixture. Place the last sponge layer on top. Chill in the fridge for 2 hours. Cut the cake vertically into slices and dust these lightly with icing sugar and flakes of milk chocolate before serving.

Milk, with or without vanilla essence for flavouring, can be used to moisten the sponge cake layers instead of rum.

Chocolate custard–cream biscuits

*preparation **25 minutes** · cooking time **25 minutes** · easy*

250 g/9 oz plain flour
2 eggs + 1 extra egg yolk
120 g/4 oz caster sugar
130 g/4½ oz butter
1 vanilla pod
1 unwaxed orange (grated rind only)

For the filling
200 g/7 oz plain chocolate
150 ml/5 fl oz whipping cream

To decorate
icing sugar

Sift the flour into a large mixing bowl; make a well in the centre and add the lightly beaten eggs and extra yolk, the sugar, and the butter, cut into very small pieces. Combine these ingredients using your hands, adding the seeds scraped from the vanilla pod (split the pod in half lengthways and, using a smooth-bladed knife, scrape out the seeds) and the finely grated rind of the orange. Work the mixture briefly, until smooth and homogenous, shape into a ball, wrap in clingfilm and chill in the fridge for 30 minutes.

Roll out the biscuit dough into a thin sheet (½ cm/just under ¼ in thick) on a floured work surface and cut out into 30 small discs with a round pastry cutter. Place these on a non-stick baking sheet and bake in a preheated oven at 180°C/350°F/gas mark 4 for 20 minutes.

Melt the chocolate over hot water; allow it to cool a little while you whip the cream stiffly. Combine the lukewarm chocolate with the cream. When the biscuits are cold, sandwich them together in pairs with some filling between them. Dust with sifted icing sugar and serve.

You can use half the quantity of plain flour and add 100 g/3½ oz ground almonds. For a different filling, melt 200 g/7 oz plain chocolate with 90 g/3 oz butter; stir in 100 ml/3½ fl oz very strong coffee and mix with 150 ml/5 fl oz cream, whipped until stiff.

Hazelnut pastry tarts with ganache filling

*preparation **35 minutes** · cooking time **20 minutes** · easy*

75 g/scant 3 oz hazelnuts,
blanched and skinned
100 g/3½ oz caster sugar
100 g/3½ oz butter
150 g/5 oz flour, sifted
2 egg yolks
pinch of salt

For the ganache
200 g/7 oz good-quality plain chocolate
(80% cocoa solids)
80 ml/3 fl oz double cream

To decorate
coarsely chopped or slivered hazelnuts

Place the hazelnuts and sugar in a food processor and process until the nuts are finely chopped and the mixture has a sandy look to it. Cut the butter into small pieces and work it into the flour and the hazelnut and sugar mixture in a large mixing bowl using the tips of your fingers or a pastry blender. Add the egg yolks and a pinch of salt and combine briefly but thoroughly by hand. Wrap the mixture in clingfilm and chill in the fridge for 1 hour.

Roll out the pastry on a floured work surface and use it to line six greased and floured fluted tartlet tins with removable bottoms. Prick the flat surface of each uncooked pastry case with a fork and cover with baking beans. Place in a preheated oven at 180°C/350F°/gas mark 4 for about 15 minutes; unmould on to a cake rack and leave to cool upside down.

Melt the chocolate in the microwave or over hot water and whisk in the cream. Turn the tartlets the right way up and fill with the ganache. When cold, sprinkle each tartlet with some of the chopped hazelnuts.

Grinding nuts with icing sugar or caster sugar means that any oil they release is absorbed by the sugar. When processed alone and for too long, nuts heat up and develop an unpleasant aftertaste.

Milk chocolate and walnut mini brownies

*preparation **30 minutes** · cooking time **40 minutes** · fairly easy*

125 g/4½ oz milk chocolate
90 g/3 oz butter, softened
250 g/9 oz icing sugar
1 vanilla pod
2 eggs
80 g/scant 3 oz plain flour
1 heaped tsp baking powder
30 g/1 oz unsweetened cocoa powder
120 g/4 oz walnuts, coarsely chopped

Melt the chocolate over hot water or in the microwave. Cream the butter and sugar in a mixing bowl with a hand-held electric whisk until pale and fluffy, add the seeds from the vanilla pod (split the pod in half lengthways and, using a smooth-bladed knife, scrape out the seeds). Whisk in the lightly beaten eggs. Continue beating as you gradually pour in the melted chocolate.

Add the sifted flour, baking powder and cocoa powder, using a mixing spatula. Stir in the chopped walnuts. Line a greased 28- x 18-cm/11- x 7-in cake tin with baking paper and turn the brownie mixture into it, smoothing the surface level. Bake in a preheated oven at 180°C/350°F/gas mark 4 for about 35 minutes.

Allow to cool before cutting into small squares. Serve as petits fours in little paper cases.

These famous American favourites can also be served hot with vanilla ice cream. This quantity should yield approximately 22 mini brownies.

Hazelnut mocha cake

*preparation **25 minutes** · cooking time **50 minutes** · easy*

300 g/10 oz hazelnuts
200 g/7 oz caster sugar
5 eggs
30 ml/1 fl oz very strong coffee
300 g/10 oz plain chocolate
100 g/3½ oz butter
2 vanilla pods
60 g/2 oz potato flour or cornflour
3 tsp baking powder

Place the hazelnuts and sugar in a food processor and process until the hazelnuts are finely ground (this is hazelnut 'flour'– see recipe for almond 'flour' on pages 18–19). Transfer to a mixing bowl and stir in the eggs and the black coffee. Melt the chocolate with the butter over hot water and, stirring constantly, gradually add it to the hazelnut mixture.

Add the vanilla seeds, scraped from the vanilla pod (split the pod in half lengthways and, using a smooth-bladed knife, scrape out the seeds), then stir in the sifted flour and baking powder. Mix gently but thoroughly. Transfer to a greased and floured 20-cm/8-in cake tin and bake in a preheated oven at 180°C/350°F/gas mark 4 for 50 minutes.

Serve the cake with a cappuccino and add a dusting of icing sugar if wished.

You may choose to melt the chocolate with the butter in a microwave on a medium setting: stir frequently and make sure it does not approach boiling point.

Chocolate coconut brownies

*preparation **30 minutes** • cooking time **35 minutes** • easy*

120 g/4 oz plain chocolate
90 g/3 oz butter
2 eggs
200 g/7 oz caster sugar
90 g/3 oz plain flour
30 g/1 oz desiccated coconut

Break the chocolate into small pieces and melt it with the butter over hot water; remove from the heat and transfer to a mixing bowl to cool down.

Whisk the eggs with the sugar until light and pale; mix with the chocolate and then stir in the sifted flour, followed by the desiccated coconut.

Grease a 20-cm/8-in square cake tin with a little butter. Transfer the cake mixture to the tin and bake in a preheated oven at 180°C/350°F/gas mark 4 for about 30 minutes, by which time the surface of the cake should be crisp and crunchy with the inside still fairly moist and soft. When cold, cut the cake into squares.

*You can serve these cakes with a fruit sauce made by heating
150 g/5 oz blackberries or mulberries in a frying pan with 2 tbsp caster sugar for
5–7 minutes, shaking the pan frequently.*

Milk chocolate and walnut carrot cake

*preparation **30 minutes** · cooking time **45 minutes** · easy*

5 eggs
150 g/5 oz caster sugar
150 g/5 oz plain flour
40 g/1½ oz unsweetened cocoa powder
175 g/6 oz peeled carrots, grated
50 g/2 oz walnuts, coarsely chopped
50 ml/2 fl oz sunflower oil

For the filling
175 g/6 oz milk chocolate
350 g/12 oz mascarpone
175 g/6 oz icing sugar

Brush a 20-cm/8-in cake tin lightly with oil and line with baking paper. Whisk the eggs with the sugar in a mixing bowl over hot water using a hand-held electric or balloon whisk until the mixture has increased in volume and thickened.

Remove the bowl from the heat and continue whisking until cool. Stir in the sifted flour and cocoa powder, followed by the carrots, walnuts and the oil. Transfer this mixture into the cake tin, place in a preheated oven and bake at 180°C/350°F/gas mark 4 for 45 minutes or until well risen. While the cake is baking, melt the milk chocolate over hot water; mix the mascarpone with the icing sugar and stir in the melted chocolate.

Cut the cake horizontally in half when it has cooled and fill with half the chocolate mascarpone mixture; use the remaining half as a topping, drawing it into small peaks. Chill in the fridge for 20 minutes before serving.

You can substitute blanched, skinned and chopped almonds for the walnuts for a subtle alteration in taste.

Chocolate and almond layer biscuits

*preparation **50 minutes** · cooking time **20 minutes** · easy*

500 g/generous 1 lb plain flour
100 g/3½ oz caster sugar
100 g/3½ oz butter, melted
150 g/5 oz runny honey
80 ml/3 fl oz Amaretto liqueur
3 egg yolks
1 unwaxed orange (juice only, strained)
sunflower oil, for frying
150 g/5 oz plain chocolate
80 g/3 oz toasted almonds, chopped
a little thick honey (optional)

Place the flour and sugar in a mixing bowl, make a well in the centre and pour in the melted butter and the honey: work the butter quickly into this mixture by hand, adding the Amaretto liqueur. Add the egg yolks, followed by the orange juice, a little at a time. As soon as the mixture is smooth and homogenous, roll out into a fairly thick sheet and cut out 30–40 little discs with a small round pastry cutter. Fry these in sunflower oil for a few minutes before removing carefully and draining on kitchen paper.

Melt the chocolate over hot water. Spread a little chocolate over a biscuit and press another on top. Repeat with the remaining biscuits. Roll the edges of the sandwiched biscuits in the chopped almonds which will stick to the edges of the chocolate filling. Drizzle a little honey on the top of each biscuit if wished.

You can bake these biscuits instead of frying them, in a preheated oven at 180°C/350°F/gas mark 4 for about 10 minutes.

Steamed chocolate soufflés

*preparation **30 minutes** · cooking time **20 minutes** · easy*

180 g/6 oz plain flour
20 g/scant 1 oz unsweetened cocoa powder
1 tsp baking powder
pinch of salt
1 egg
80 g/3 oz caster sugar
30 g/1 oz butter, melted
50 g/2 oz raspberry jam or jelly
125 ml/4½ fl oz full-cream milk

Sift the flour, cocoa powder, baking powder and salt into a mixing bowl. Whisk the egg in another large mixing bowl with the sugar until pale and frothy; stir in the melted butter and jam or jelly. Gradually add the flour mixture to the egg mixture, alternating additions of flour with the milk. The mixture should be thick and smooth.

Spoon the soufflé mixture into eight–ten greased ramekins or any small, deep and heatproof receptacles. Pour a little water into a pressure cooker; place the ramekins in this. Close the pressure cooker and cook the soufflés for 20 minutes after the whistle starts to sound indicating the cooker has reached the correct pressure.

Remove the ramekins and allow the soufflés to cool, then chill in the fridge until just before they are served. Fresh raspberries go well with these.

You can serve a hot custard drizzled over the soufflés (see recipe on page 78) and a few raspberries for decoration.

Chocolate almond cakes with redcurrants

*preparation **30 minutes** • cooking time **20 minutes** • easy*

75 g/scant 3 oz blanched, skinned almonds
100 g/3½ oz milk chocolate, in small pieces
50 g/2 oz plain chocolate, in small pieces
75 g/scant 3 oz butter, softened
75 g/scant 3 oz caster sugar
15 ml/1 tbsp brandy
2 eggs
100 g/3½ oz mascarpone
40 g/1½ oz plain flour, sifted
10 g/1 tbsp potato flour or cornflour

To decorate
200 g/7 oz white chocolate
7 g/¼ oz leaf gelatine, soaked in
cold water, blotted dry
1 egg + 1 extra yolk
120 g/4 oz caster sugar
150 ml/5 fl oz whipping cream
fresh redcurrants

Toast the almonds lightly in the oven at 160°C/325°F/gas mark 3 then chop finely in a food processor. Melt both chocolates together over hot water. Beat the butter and sugar with a hand-held electric or balloon whisk until pale and creamy.

Combine the butter and sugar mixture with the melted chocolate, brandy, lightly beaten eggs and mascarpone in this order. Stir in the almonds and the plain flour, sifted with the corn- or potato flour. Grease 20–30 small (individual) rectangular cake tins and fill these two-thirds full with the mixture. Bake in a preheated oven at 180°C/350°F/gas mark 4 for about 20 minutes. Allow to cool before turning out.

Melt the white chocolate over hot water with the leaf gelatine; remove from the heat. Beat the egg and extra yolk with the sugar until pale and fluffy; combine with the chocolate. Fold in the stiffly whipped cream and chill this topping in the fridge until firm enough to pipe on top of the cakes. Decorate with trimmed redcurrants.

Tartlets with chocolate custard and marrons glacés

*preparation **30 minutes** · cooking time **10 minutes** · fairly easy*

1 egg + **2** extra yolks
20 g/scant 1 oz caster sugar
10 ml/scant 1 tbsp rum
70 g/2½ oz plain chocolate
50 g/2 oz gianduia or praline chocolate
120 g/4 oz marrons glacés or tinned sweetened
chestnut purée
200 ml/7 fl oz whipping cream
300 g/10 oz Viennese sweet pastry (see page 26)

To decorate
unsweetened cocoa powder

Whisk the eggs and the extra yolks with the sugar and rum in a bowl over hot water until the mixture has increased in volume and thickened. Melt the two types of chocolate in the microwave or over hot water and combine with the egg mixture away from the heat. Stir in the marrons glacés (if whole or in pieces, crush them into a purée).

Fold in the stiffly whipped cream. Cover with clingfilm and place briefly in the freezer; when firm, transfer to the fridge.

Roll out the pastry (see recipe on page 26) into a thin sheet and use it to line 30–35 small greased tartlet tins; bake in a preheated oven at 180°C/350°F/gas mark 4 for 10 minutes and allow to cool; unmould. Fill each tartlet with the chocolate and sweet chestnut filling, sprinkling with a little sifted cocoa powder. Serve slightly chilled.

Various liqueurs can be substituted for the rum, or pure vanilla essence can be used to flavour the filling before it is folded into the cream. Tinned sweetened chestnut purée is usually flavoured with vanilla.

Hazelnut and white chocolate biscuits

*preparation **30 minutes** · cooking time **20 minutes** · easy*

125 g/4½ oz butter, softened
125 g/4½ oz caster sugar
2 egg yolks
60 g/2 oz finely chopped hazelnuts
155 g/5 oz plain flour
110 g/4 oz very fine polenta or cornmeal
pinch of bicarbonate of soda
40 g/1½ oz white chocolate, finely chopped

To decorate
20 best-quality hazelnuts

Beat the softened butter with the sugar until very pale and creamy, stir in the egg yolks. Add the finely chopped hazelnuts and then stir in the flour and polenta, sifted together with the bicarbonate of soda, adding a little at a time. Work the mixture only just enough to blend the ingredients; press it out between two sheets of cellophane paper or clingfilm and chill for 1 hour in the fridge.

Add the finely chopped chocolate to the biscuit mixture, working them in evenly; shape into a ball and chill for a further 20–30 minutes. Roll out into a fairly thick sheet between two fresh sheets of greaseproof paper and use pastry cutters to cut out 20–25 oval or scalloped biscuit shapes. Place these on a baking tray covered with greaseproof paper and press a hazelnut into the centre of each biscuit. Bake in a preheated oven at 170°C/325°F/gas mark 3 for about 20 minutes. Allow to cool before serving.

Buy the best and freshest hazelnuts you can find to decorate these biscuits, as the flavour will be so much better.

Desserts and after-dinner treats

The best time of the day for relaxing

with friends and loved ones, when you

can forget all about your busy life and share

delicious treats that appeal to at least four

of the five senses...

Chocolate cups with lemon cream and fruit

by Omar Busi

*preparation **20 minutes** • cooking time **10 minutes** • fairly easy*

60 ml/generous 2 fl oz lemon juice, strained
½ unwaxed lemon (grated rind only)
250 g/9 oz butter
200 g/7 oz icing sugar
1 egg + 5 egg yolks

To decorate and serve
30–35 small plain-chocolate cupcake cases (see method)
red berries, kiwi fruit, fresh mint leaves

Heat the lemon juice, grated lemon rind, butter and sugar in a saucepan; bring to the boil. Remove from the heat. Place the egg and yolks in a bowl over hot water and whisk while adding the warm lemon mixture in a thin stream. Continue whisking over hot water. As soon as the mixture thickens (this happens at 85°C/185°F), remove immediately from the heat.

Pour without delay into a wide, cold bowl to stop the eggs cooking further; chill in the fridge, then process briefly with a blender. Fill little chocolate cases with this lemon custard and decorate with pieces of fruit and small mint leaves.

Make the chocolate cases yourself if you cannot buy them: temper the chocolate using one of the methods shown on pages 90–95 and coat the insides of silicone moulds (you can buy these from specialist patisserie equipment suppliers' shops or online). After 2 minutes turn the moulds upside down to drain off any excess chocolate and use a spatula to eliminate any overruns.

Place the moulds in the fridge, upside down inside a large, dry, airtight plastic container; leave for 20–30 minutes to harden. Carefully unmould the chocolate cases.

Strawberry and chocolate timbales

*preparation **25 minutes** · cooking time **10 minutes** · easy*

300 g/10 oz strawberries
60 g/2 oz plain chocolate
70 g/2½ oz gianduia or praline chocolate
100 ml/3½ fl oz very thick cream

Rinse the strawberries, pat dry and hull them before cutting into fairly small pieces.

Place both types of chocolate in a bowl with the cream and melt over hot water or in the microwave. Stir briefly as soon as the chocolate has melted and allow to cool.

Divide the strawberries into four equal portions, reserving four to eight pieces for decoration; place four small cylindrical moulds (without bases) in a flat container and pack a layer of strawberries into each mould. Pour a quarter of the chocolate cream into each mould and chill for 1 hour and then transfer to the freezer for 1 hour. Unmould and serve.

You can mix very thin shreds of fresh mint leaves with the strawberries for extra flavour. Avoid sweetening the strawberries as this will make them release a lot of juice.

Rum and cocoa wafer baskets with mascarpone filling

*preparation **30 minutes** · cooking time **5 minutes** · easy*

1 egg white
80 g/3 oz vanilla sugar (see page 20)
1 tbsp dark rum
80 g/3 oz butter, melted
80 g/3 oz plain flour, sifted
20 g/scant 1 oz unsweetened cocoa powder

For the filling
120 g/4 oz mascarpone
100 g/3½ oz spreadable cream cheese
(very fresh ricotta or similar)
15 g/1½ tbsp icing sugar
1 tsp vanilla essence

To decorate
150 g/5 oz raspberries
fresh mint leaves

Whisk the egg white in a small bowl with the vanilla sugar until stiff; whisk in the rum and the melted butter. Stir in the sifted flour and cocoa powder briefly: the mixture should be fairly thick and elastic. Chill in the fridge for 20 minutes.

Place sheets of baking paper on baking trays; spoon a little chilled mixture on to the paper; use the back of the spoon to spread out into a disc of 5 cm/2 in diameter. Repeat until all the mixture is used up. Bake in a preheated oven at 200°C/400°F/gas mark 6 for 5 minutes. Have several little cylindrical moulds ready, turned upside down on the work surface. As soon as you remove the wafers from the oven place them over the moulds and keep squeezing their lower edges gently against the mould to shape them into little 'baskets'.

Beat the mascarpone and cream cheese with the icing sugar (use a little vanilla essence if you have no vanilla sugar). Spoon into the baskets, decorating each one with a raspberry and a mint leaf. Serve at once.

Little chocolate bavarois with meringue

*preparation **20 minutes** · cooking time **10 minutes** · easy*

200 ml/7 fl oz full-cream milk
1 vanilla pod
3 egg yolks
30 g/1 oz unsweetened cocoa powder
80 g/3 oz caster sugar
10 g/scant ½ oz leaf gelatine
150 ml/5 fl oz whipping cream
40 g/1½ oz crumbled meringues

Heat the milk very slowly with the vanilla pod in it. Whisk the egg yolks in a bowl with the cocoa powder and sugar. When the milk reaches boiling point, remove the vanilla pod, split it in half lengthways using a smooth-bladed knife and scrape out the seeds; add these to the hot milk. Continue whisking the egg mixture as you add the hot milk in a thin stream.

Squeeze any excess moisture out of the soaked and softened leaf gelatine and allow it to dissolve completely in the hot custard mixture; allow to cool a little before folding in the stiffly whipped cream.

Sprinkle the meringue into six moulds or ramekins and fill with the custard. Chill in the fridge to set. Shortly before serving, run a knife around the edge of each bavarois and turn out on to individual plates.

As a finishing touch, sprinkle the bavarois with chopped toasted almonds.

Mini milk chocolate charlottes

*preparation **40 minutes** · cooking time **5 minutes** · fairly easy*

40 ml/1½ fl oz orange flower liqueur or
orange flower water
20 sponge fingers
150 g/5 oz granulated or caster sugar
230 g/8 oz milk chocolate
150 ml/5 fl oz double cream
3 egg whites
pinch of salt
4 egg yolks

Line four small spring-release moulds with baking paper. Dilute the liqueur with a little cold water. Place the sponge fingers on a plate and sprinkle them with the diluted liqueur. Trim the sponge fingers to the height of the moulds and use them to line the sides of the moulds spaced out to allow the mousse mixture to show through.

Make a sugar syrup by boiling the sugar with about 75 ml/3 fl oz water. Melt the chocolate in the microwave or over hot water and stir in the cream. Whisk the egg whites stiffly with a pinch of salt and continue whisking as you add the sugar syrup in a thin stream.

Stir the egg yolks into the chocolate cream. Fold this mixture into the meringue and fill the moulds with it. Chill in the fridge overnight. Unmould the mini charlottes carefully before serving.

You could also dip the sponge fingers in your favourite liqueur or coffee to moisten and flavour them.

Little chocolate puddings with soft centres

*preparation **30 minutes** · cooking time **15 minutes** · easy*

100 g/3½ oz plain chocolate, in small pieces
100 g/3½ oz butter
2 eggs
80 g/3 oz caster sugar
30 g/1 oz plain flour

Melt the chocolate and butter over hot water; stir and leave to cool while you whisk the eggs and sugar until pale and fluffy; stir in the sifted flour a little at a time.

Add the melted chocolate and butter to the mixture, stirring well.

Grease four ramekin dishes and spoon in the chocolate mixture. Place in a preheated oven and bake at 200°C/400°F/gas mark 6 for about 10 minutes, checking frequently after the first five minutes. The top and sides should be well cooked but the centre should remain soft. Take out of the oven and serve immediately.

You can vary this recipe by using milk chocolate, gianduia or praline chocolate: this will be sweetened, so use 15–20 g/½–1 oz less sugar.

Chocolate and marron glacé soufflé

*preparation **30 minutes** • cooking time **15 minutes** • fairly easy*

3 egg whites
25 g/1 oz caster sugar
300 g/10 oz plain chocolate
150 ml/5 fl oz full-cream milk
4 egg yolks
150 g/5 oz marrons glacés, crumbled
20 g/scant 1 oz slivered almonds

To decorate
icing sugar

Whisk the egg whites stiffly with the caster sugar. Place the chocolate and milk in the top of a double-boiler and heat gently until the chocolate has melted; allow to cool before adding the egg yolks a little at a time, stirring continuously. Fold this mixture into the egg whites gently but thoroughly, keeping as much air in them as possible. Add the crumbled marrons glacés.

Grease eight–ten individual soufflé dishes, fill them with the chocolate soufflé mixture and sprinkle a few slivered almonds on top of each one. Bake in a preheated oven at 180°C/350°F/gas mark 4 for about 15 minutes (longer than usual: they need to cook through).

Take the soufflés out of the oven when they are cooked and cool completely before unmoulding them. Serve with a dusting of sifted icing sugar over them.

Coarsely chopped dried fruit can be substituted for marrons glacés: soft dates, prunes, figs or apricots. You can also add chopped almonds, hazelnuts, walnuts to the mixture or sprinkle them over the soufflés as a topping. Soufflés always have to be placed in a preheated oven: leave the inner glass door closed if you have to check on them.

Milk chocolate and almond puddings

*preparation **35 minutes** · cooking time **30 minutes** · easy*

150 g/5 oz almonds, blanched and skinned
50 g/2 oz brioche or any sweet yeast bread
200 g/7oz milk chocolate
100 g/3½ oz plain chocolate
35 ml/generous 1 fl oz brandy
150 g/5 oz butter, softened
150 g/5 oz sugar
4 eggs
1 vanilla pod
200 g/7 oz mascarpone
a little unsweetened cocoa powder

Toast the almonds lightly in the oven at 160°C/325°F/gas mark 3 for a few minutes until pale golden brown. Chop them fairly finely, with the brioche, in a food processor. Grease four 10-cm/4-in diameter deep moulds with butter and sprinkle the almond and brioche mixture all over their insides, tipping out and reserving the excess. Melt both types of chocolate together in the microwave, add the brandy and stir until the mixture is lukewarm and has thickened a little.

Beat the butter and sugar together until pale. Beat in the chocolate and then the eggs, adding these a little at a time. Split the vanilla pod in half lengthways and, using a smooth-bladed knife, scrape out the seeds; stir these into the mixture. Mix in the mascarpone.

Stir in the remaining almond and brioche mixture and divide between the two moulds. Bake in a preheated oven at 170°C/340°F/gas mark 4 for about 20–25 minutes. Allow to cool for 10 minutes before unmoulding, then sprinkle with the sifted cocoa powder. Serve immediately, with a little whipped cream if wished.

Any sweet yeast cake can be used for this recipe, preferably a little stale: the Italian panettone or pandoro would be suitable, or any similar sweet yeast bread.

Carrot and coconut cake with milk chocolate icing

*preparation **30 minutes** · cooking **50 minutes** · easy*

300 g/10 oz carrots, peeled
150 g/5 oz almonds, blanched and skinned
150 g/5 oz caster sugar
150 g/5 oz coconut flour
3 tsp baking powder
3 eggs

For the icing
200 g/7 oz milk chocolate
desiccated coconut (optional)

Process the carrots in a food processor until very finely chopped indeed (or grate them very finely); transfer to a mixing bowl. Grind the almonds finely with the sugar in the food processor and stir into the carrots. Add the sifted coconut flour and baking powder in instalments, alternating with the lightly beaten eggs and stirring with a wooden spoon. Turn into a greased 24-cm/9½-in cake tin.

Bake in a preheated oven at 160°C/325°F/gas mark 3 for 10 minutes, then increase the oven temperature to 180°C/350°F/gas mark 4 and bake for a further 40 minutes. Remove from the oven and allow to cool.

Melt the chocolate over hot water and spread it all over the cake, smoothing it with a palette knife. Allow the chocolate to set before serving, and dust the finished cake with a little desiccated coconut if wished.

You can also bake this cake in a rectangular cake tin. This is a very light, gluten-free cake which can be enjoyed at any time of day, even at breakfast time. Coconut flour is available in specialist shops and online.

Whisky and chocolate truffles

by Omar Busi

*preparation **25 minutes** • cooking time **5 minutes** • easy*

300 ml/10 fl oz double cream
500 g/generous 1 lb good-quality
plain chocolate (64% cocoa solids)
100 g/3½ oz runny honey
130 g/4½ oz butter, softened
80 ml/3 fl oz whisky
unsweetened cocoa powder

Heat the cream gently in a small saucepan until lukewarm. Place the chocolate in the microwave and heat until it has barely melted. Remove from the microwave and add the warm cream in a thin stream while stirring gently. Stir in the honey, followed by the butter and, finally, the whisky. Chill in the fridge for about 1 hour.

While the chocolate ganache is cooling, take it out of the fridge at frequent intervals and stir thoroughly with a mixing spatula to make it smooth and homogenous. Just before using the ganache, stir it thoroughly to ensure that some of it (for instance, around the sides of the bowl) is not colder and thicker than the rest. Sift plenty of cocoa powder on to a large, wide plate.

Transfer the ganache to a piping bag with a large, plain nozzle and pipe out 30–40 short lengths, cutting these off from the nozzle opening with a knife repeatedly dipped in iced water and allowing them to fall directly on to the cocoa powder.

Using your hands and working as quickly as possible, roll the pieces around in the cocoa, shaping them into little balls; place them on a large plate covered with greaseproof paper and return them to the fridge where they should chill for at least 3 hours. When they are cold, roll them again in cocoa powder if necessary and serve.

*You can flavour the milk as you heat it with mint leaves or a cinnamon stick.
Do this a day in advance and leave the milk in the fridge overnight,
covered with clingfilm. Strain and use as above.*

Mint and chocolate cake

*preparation **25 minutes** • cooking time **45 minutes** • easy*

100 g/3½ oz butter
250 g/9 oz caster sugar
3 eggs
250 g/9 oz very fresh ricotta cheese
250 g/9 oz plain flour
5 tsp baking powder
80 g/3 oz chocolate chips
120 ml/4 fl oz mint syrup
pinch of salt

To decorate
150 g/5 oz chocolate and hazelnut spread
(see page 82)
50g/2 oz flaked almonds

Beat the butter with the sugar until soft and pale; continue beating as you add the eggs one at a time. Stir in the ricotta thoroughly, followed by the sifted flour and baking powder and the chocolate chips. Lastly, add the mint syrup and a pinch of salt.

Transfer the mixture to a 23-cm/9-in cake tin, greased with butter and dusted with flour, and bake in a preheated oven at 190°C/375°F/gas mark 5 for about 45 minutes.

Take the cake out of the oven and leave to cool. When cold, top with the chocolate and hazelnut spread and sprinkle with the flaked almonds.

You can use this recipe to make individual cakes; grease little cake tins, dust them with flour and halve the baking time.

Pear and white chocolate cake

*preparation **40 minutes** · cooking time **65 minutes** · fairly easy*

100 g/3½ oz white chocolate
2 firm, ripe pears
165 g/5½ oz cane sugar
30 ml/1 fl oz grappa
3 eggs
250 g/9 oz plain flour
3 tsp baking powder
120 g/4 oz butter, melted
100 ml/3½ fl oz single cream,
at room temperature

For the caramel
100 g/3½ oz granulated or caster sugar
40 ml/1½ fl oz water

To make the caramel, heat the sugar and water in a small saucepan over a medium heat until it caramelises (do not allow it to thicken or darken too much). Use a spoon to sprinkle enough caramel into the bottom of a deep, round 23-cm/9-in cake tin to cover it completely. Set aside to cool.

Melt the chocolate over hot water or in the microwave. Peel the pears and slice them into a bowl; sprinkle them with the cane sugar and the grappa. Stir in the lightly beaten eggs and the sifted flour and baking powder.

Add the melted butter followed by the cream and, finally, the melted chocolate. Stir well. Spoon this mixture into the cake tin and bake in a preheated oven at 180°C/350°F/gas mark 4 for about 1 hour. Allow to cool before serving.

If you have any caramel left over, you can use it to decorate the plates on which the cake is served.

Cocoa tartlets with ricotta topping

*preparation **30 minutes** · cooking time **10 minutes** · easy*

400 g/14 oz plain flour
100 g/3½ oz unsweetened cocoa powder
240 g/8½ oz icing sugar
250 g/9 oz butter, chilled and cut
into small pieces
5 egg yolks
200 g/7 oz very fresh ricotta cheese
½ vanilla pod
fresh mint leave, to serve

Place the sifted flour, cocoa and 200 g/7 oz of the icing sugar in a food processor with the butter and process until blended into a mixture with the appearance of very fine breadcrumbs. Continue to process in short bursts as you gradually add the egg yolks. Use your fingertips to lift the mixture out of the processor; shape it into a ball, wrap in clingfilm and chill in the fridge for about 1 hour.

Roll out the mixture between two sheets of greaseproof paper. Grease four fluted or plain tartlet moulds. Cut the pastry into rounds big enough to line the moulds neatly. Prick the bottom of the pastry with a fork. Bake in a preheated oven at 180°C/350°F/gas mark 4 for about 10 minutes. Unmould when cold.

Push the ricotta through a sieve into a bowl; add the remaining icing sugar and the seeds scraped from the vanilla pod (split the pod in half lengthways and, using a smooth-bladed knife, scrape out the seeds). Mix very well.

To serve, turn the tartlets upside down and top each one with a quenelle of the ricotta mixture and a very small fresh mint leaf.

For a filling that is even quicker and simpler to prepare, use 100 ml/3½ fl oz whipping cream, whipped until stiff, sweetened and flavoured, instead of the ricotta.

Mocha cake

*preparation **25 minutes** · cooking time **35 minutes** · easy*

120 g/4 oz butter, softened
100 g/3½ oz sugar
2 eggs
100 g/3½ oz plain flour
60 g/2 oz unsweetened cocoa powder
3 tsp baking powder
pinch of salt
15–20 ml/1–1½ tbsp milk
100 ml/3½ fl oz black coffee

Process the softened butter with the sugar (reserving 1 tablespoon for later) at low speed in a food processor until pale and frothy. Transfer to a mixing bowl and add the lightly beaten eggs. Using a wooden spoon, stir in the flour in batches, sifted with 40 g/1½ oz of the cocoa powder, the baking powder and a pinch of salt; lastly add the milk.

Transfer the cake mixture to a greased, straight-sided ovenproof pie or soufflé dish or cake tin. Mix the remaining cocoa and the reserved sugar and sprinkle evenly over the top; sprinkle the surface with all the cold coffee. Bake in a preheated oven at 180°C/350°F/gas mark 4 for 30–35 minutes.

Turn out the cake and slice before serving, sprinkling a little of the coffee residue from the bottom of the dish over each slice. This should make about 8 servings.

This cake mixture can be baked in individual portions, using ramekins or similar small ovenproof dishes (but remember to halve the cooking time).

Trifle with red berries and white chocolate custard

*preparation **25 minutes** · cooking **30 minutes** · easy*

4 egg yolks
80 g/3 oz caster sugar
30 g/generous 1 oz plain flour
10 g/1 tbsp potato flour or cornflour
350 ml/12 fl oz full-cream milk
150 ml/5 fl oz single cream
½ vanilla pod
100 g/3½ oz white chocolate, in small pieces
½ unwaxed orange (grated rind only)
16 sponge fingers
200 g/7 oz assorted red berries

For the syrup
60 g/generous 2 oz granulated or caster sugar
200 ml/7 fl oz water
4 mint leaves
pinch of star anise powder
½ orange (juice only)
20 ml/1–1½ tbsp mandarin liqueur

Whisk the egg yolks and sugar until pale and fluffy; stir in the sifted flour and potato flour or cornflour.

Heat the milk and cream slowly with the half the vanilla pod in it to 80°C/175°F; whisk the egg, sugar and flour mixture in a separate sauce pan while you add the hot milk in a thin stream (having removed the vanilla pod). Cook while stirring continuously over a low heat until the custard thickens. Take off the heat and add the chocolate; allow this to melt before stirring in the orange rind.

Make the syrup by boiling the sugar and water until the syrup reaches 120°C/245°F; allow to cool a little. Stir in the mint, star anise, orange juice and mandarin liqueur. When the syrup is cold, dip the sponge fingers in it and use them to line a shallow serving dish (big enough to make 4–6 servings). Pour in one third of the custard and sprinkle with half the red fruits. Repeat this layering, ending with a layer of custard.

Potato flour is now fairly widely available and has many uses. It is particularly useful for desserts, cakes and some sauces. Cornflour can be used instead.

White chocolate mousse with lemon jelly

*preparation **25 minutes** · cooking time **10 minutes** · fairly easy*

250 g/9 oz white chocolate, coarsely chopped
150 ml/5 fl oz whipping cream
1 unwaxed lemon
10 g/scant ½ oz leaf gelatine
2 egg whites
pinch of salt

For the jelly
2 unwaxed lemons (juice and grated rind)
1 tbsp caster sugar
5 g/¼ oz leaf gelatine, soaked in cold water

Melt the chopped chocolate over hot water or in the microwave. Whisk the cream until stiff in a separate bowl. Finely grate the rind of the lemon and mix this with it's strained juice. Heat the lemon juice and rind very gently and add the gelatine (squeezed free of any excess water) to dissolve it.

Combine the melted chocolate with the whipped cream and leave until lukewarm; stir in the lemon mixture. Whisk the egg whites stiffly with a pinch of salt and fold into the mixture. Transfer the mixture to a serving bowl and cover with clingfilm. Allow to set in the fridge for 3–4 hours.

Squeeze the lemon juice for the jelly, strain it and add 15 ml/½ fl oz water and the sugar. Heat this liquid slowly with the gelatine in a small saucepan until the gelatine has dissolved. Strain once more and pour into one or more flexible moulds (silicone if possible). Allow to set in the fridge. Spoon the mousse on to individual plates, accompanied by the chopped jelly. This should make about 4 servings.

This fresh and delicate combination makes an ideal summer dessert. Try it with fresh blueberries, strawberries or raspberries.

Bitter chocolate melting slices

*preparation **25 minutes** · cooking time **30 minutes** · easy*

250 g/9 oz good-quality plain chocolate
(70% cocoa solids)
200 g/7 oz butter
100 g/3½ oz icing sugar
4 eggs

Break the chocolate into pieces and melt it over hot water in a fairly large heatproof bowl or in a hemispherical double-boiler. Gradually add small pieces of the butter, stirring continuously. Add the sifted icing sugar a little at a time, stirring continuously. The mixture should be very smooth and well blended.

Beat in the eggs a little at a time, using a hand-held electric or a balloon whisk. Pour the mixture into a 28- x 18-cm/11- x 7-in cake tin that has been greased with butter and dusted with flour.

Bake in a preheated oven at 200°C/400°F/gas mark 6 for 25–30 minutes. Allow to cool totally before unmoulding. Cut into thick slices and serve.

*You can serve a vanilla-flavoured custard with this chocolate dessert
(see recipe on page 78).*

Mini cheesecakes

*preparation **20 minutes** · cooking time **30 minutes** · easy*

70 g/2½ oz white chocolate
240 g/8½ oz very fresh soft goat's cheese
90 ml/3 fl oz double cream
130 g/4½ oz icing sugar
1 egg
4 bitter chocolate biscuits

To decorate
raspberries
small mint leaves

Melt the chocolate over hot water or in the microwave, stirring frequently. Using a hand-held electric whisk, whisk the goat's cheese in a large bowl with the cream and icing sugar until light and frothy.

Whisk the egg over hot water until it increases in volume and thickens slightly. Fold into the cheese mixture. Stirring with a wooden spoon or a rubber mixing spatula, add the melted chocolate in a thin stream.

Line four small china ramekins with two criss-crossing strips of greaseproof paper in each. Place a biscuit in the bottom of each mould. Fill two-thirds full with the cheesecake mixture.

Bake in a preheated oven at 170°C/340°F/gas mark 3–4 for 20 minutes. Allow to cool, then chill in the fridge for 1 hour. Decorate with rinsed, dried raspberries and a few fresh mint leaves.

You could also use slices of chocolate cake, cut to size, instead of biscuits, for the base of these mini cheesecakes.

Chocolate mousse

*preparation **25 minutes** • cooking time **20 minutes** • easy*

200 g/7 oz plain chocolate
2 egg yolks
50 g/2 oz caster sugar
160 ml/5½ fl oz whipping cream
2 egg whites

Melt the chocolate over hot water. Whisk the egg yolks with the sugar in a separate bowl over hot water until they are pale and frothy; they will start to thicken at 50°C/122°F. Remove from the heat.

Combine the warm chocolate with the egg mixture in a mixing bowl then fold in the stiffly beaten cream. Fold in the stiffly beaten egg whites gently but thoroughly. Transfer the mixture to a large piping bag fitted with a large fluted nozzle.

Pipe the mousse neatly into four small glass dishes and chill in the fridge for approximately 4 hours before serving.

In this recipe the heatproof bowls containing the ingredients to be heated gently are placed over pans of barely simmering water or in the top of a double-boiler and are heated by steam.

Tiramisù with strawberries and white chocolate

*preparation **20 minutes** · cooking time **10 minutes** · easy*

30 ml/2 fl oz very strong coffee
400 ml/14 fl oz water
200 g/7 oz caster sugar
200 g/7 oz sponge fingers
240 g/8 oz strawberries
3 eggs
150 g/5 oz mascarpone
110 g/4 oz white chocolate

Heat the strong coffee gently in a wide saucepan with the water and half the sugar, stirring until the sugar has completely dissolved (do not allow to boil). Allow the sweetened coffee mixture to cool a little and then dip the sponge fingers in it one by one, placing some of them in four individual serving dishes as a bottom layer. Cover with a thin layer of sliced or coarsely chopped strawberries.

Whisk the eggs with a hand-held electric or balloon whisk over hot water until pale and frothy; whisk in the mascarpone and the remaining sugar. Remove from the heat. Melt the chocolate over hot water and whisk into the egg and mascarpone mixture. Spoon half of this custard into the individual dishes followed by a layer of sliced or coarsely chopped strawberries.

Continue assembling the dessert with another layer of coffee-flavoured sponge fingers, another layer of strawberries, the remaining custard and a final topping of strawberries. Decorate with mint leaves and/or chocolate flakes if wished.

Raspberries or blackberries can be used to very good effect instead of strawberries for this delicious version of an old favourite.

Milk chocolate and rum bavarois

*preparation **30 minutes** • cooking time **15 minutes** • easy*

300 ml/10 fl oz full-cream milk
200 ml/7 fl oz double cream
60 g/2 oz egg yolk
80 g/3 oz caster sugar
15 ml/1 tbsp best-quality Navy rum
20 g/scant 1 oz unsweetened cocoa powder
200 g/7 oz milk chocolate, chopped
10 g/¼ oz leaf gelatine, soaked in cold water

Heat the milk and cream to boiling point in a saucepan over a gentle heat. Whisk the egg yolks with the sugar until pale and fluffy; whisk in the rum and the sifted cocoa powder. When the milk and cream have reached boiling point, remove from the heat and add the chocolate. Stir as the chocolate melts.

Squeeze any excess water from the gelatine and add to the hot chocolate and milk mixture to dissolve completely. Allow to cool further before whisking into the egg and sugar mixture.

Line a 28- x 18-cm/11- x 7-in cake tin or 23-cm/9-in ring mould with clingfilm, smoothing it out. Fill with the bavarois and allow to set for at least 1 hour in the fridge. Turn out on to a serving plate.

You can decorate this bavarois with piped whipped cream or with a sweet sauce of your choice. Vanilla-flavoured custard, Sabayon sauce or a simple sauce of sieved, melted jam mixed with a complementary liqueur would all go very well.

Chocolate chilli cake

*preparation **20 minutes** • cooking time **40 minutes** • easy*

125 g/4½ oz butter
300 g/10 oz plain chocolate or couverture,
in small pieces
6 egg yolks
150 g/5 oz caster sugar
60 ml/2 fl oz grappa or brandy
pinch of chilli powder, to taste
5 egg whites

To decorate
unsweetened cocoa powder

Melt the butter with the chocolate over hot water. Whisk the egg yolks with 100 g/
3½ oz of the caster sugar until pale and greatly increased in volume. Whisk in the
melted chocolate, adding this gradually and continue whisking as you add the grappa
(or substitute) and the chilli powder.

Whisk the egg whites with the remaining sugar until stiff; fold into the chocolate
mixture gently but thoroughly. Grease a 23-cm/9-in cake tin with butter and dust
lightly with flour; transfer the cake mixture to this and bake in a preheated oven at
180°C/350°F/gas mark 4 for 30 minutes, then reduce the temperature to 120°C/250°F/
gas mark ½ and continue cooking for a further 10 minutes.

Turn off the oven and leave the cake in it to 'rest' for 5–10 minutes before tuning it out
on to a cake rack and allowing it to cool. Sprinkle with a generous dusting of sifted
cocoa powder before serving.

*Couverture is high-quality chocolate, containing extra cocoa butter. It is available to buy on
the internet. Chilli powder is often used with chocolate nowadays. Piment d'Espelette is
milder than chilli powder; you can also use paprika if preferred.*

Chocolate pie

*preparation **35 minutes** • cooking time **30 minutes** • easy*

250 g/9 oz plain flour	**For the filling**
3 tsp baking powder	150 g/5 oz plain chocolate
150 g/5oz caster sugar	1 egg
1 egg + **1** extra yolk	120 g/4 oz caster sugar
150 g/5 oz butter, softened	50 ml/2 fl oz crème fraîche or double cream
1 vanilla pod	1 vanilla pod
1 unwaxed lemon (grated rind only)	

Sift the flour and baking powder into a large mixing bowl; stir in the sugar. Make a well in the centre and in it place the egg and the extra egg yolk, the butter, cut into small pieces, the seeds from the vanilla pod (split the pod in half lengthways and, using a smooth-bladed knife, scrape out the seeds) and the finely grated lemon rind. Using a pastry blender or your fingertips, work the mixture just enough to mix well and make it homogenous. Shape into a ball, cover with clingfilm and chill in the fridge for at least 30 minutes.

Melt the chocolate for the filling over hot water. Once it has melted, remove from the heat and allow to cool down. Whisk the egg with the sugar until pale and greatly increased in volume. Stir in the crème fraîche or cream and the seeds from the vanilla pod. Mix the melted chocolate into this mixture evenly and thoroughly.

Roll out just over half the chilled sweet pastry into a fairly thick sheet and use to line a greased, floured 23-cm/9-in flan tin. Fill this case with the chocolate mixture. Cover with a closely woven lattice of strips cut from the remaining pastry. Bake in a preheated oven at 160°C/325°F/gas mark 3 for about 30 minutes or until cooked through and pale golden brown. Take the pie out of the oven, and leave to cool completely before slicing and serving.

Chocolate puddings with soft strawberry centres

*preparation **30 minutes** · cooking time **15 minutes** · fairly easy*

50 g/2 oz 70% cocoa solids plain chocolate
20 ml/generous 1 tbsp double cream
70 g/2½ oz best-quality strawberry jam
100 g/3½ oz 50% cocoa solids plain chocolate
or couverture
80 g/3 oz butter
2 eggs
70 g/2½ oz caster sugar
200 g/7 oz plain flour

Melt the 70% cocoa solids chocolate with the cream over hot water; when melted, stir in the strawberry jam. Transfer into a small, deep, freezer-proof dish, cover with clingfilm or a lid and freeze until solid. Melt the 50% cocoa solids chocolate over hot water with the butter; stir and leave to cool.

Whisk the eggs with the sugar using a hand-held electric or a balloon whisk until pale and frothy; whisk in the sifted flour, adding a little at a time. When the mixture forms a ribbon when the whisk is lifted above the bowl, gently stir in the melted chocolate and butter mixture.

Transfer the mixture to four individual non-stick moulds, filling them two-thirds full; place a small ball or scoop of the frozen strawberry and chocolate mixture in each, cover quickly with the remaining mixture and bake in a preheated oven at 200°C/400°F/gas mark 6 for about 12 minutes. Allow to cool a little; unmould carefully while still warm and serve at once.

As a change, you can substitute tinned sweetened chestnut purée or chocolate and hazelnut spread (see page 82) to mix with the chocolate and cream for this dessert's soft centre. For a surprise effect, use white chocolate mixed with the cream for the filling.

Individual chocolate bonêt puddings

*preparation **30 minutes** · cooking time **50 minutes** · fairly easy*

500 ml/18 fl oz full-cream milk
50 g/2 oz sponge fingers
60 g/generous 2 oz small amaretti biscuits
15 ml/1 tbsp very strong coffee
10 g/½ oz good-quality instant
coffee powder
20 ml/generous 1 tbsp rum
20 ml/generous 1 tbsp Marsala
3 eggs
100 g/3½ oz caster sugar
25 g/1 oz unsweetened cocoa powder

Heat the milk to boiling point, then leave to cool a little. Process the sponge fingers with the amaretti biscuits in a food processor; stir the resulting very fine crumbs into the milk. Stir in the strong coffee, followed by the instant coffee powder and the rum and Marsala.

Whisk the eggs with the sugar and sifted cocoa powder until smooth and fluffy. Stir in the milk and biscuit mixture.

Coat the inside of four individual flameproof moulds or one larger flameproof mould with caramel by sprinkling a little caster sugar in the bottom and heating with care over a gas hob or in a hot oven. Make sure the caramel covers the bottom of the inside of the mould(s). Allow to cool and harden.

Fill the mould(s) with the prepared mixture and place them in a bain-marie, with hot water coming halfway up the sides of the mould(s) and cook in a preheated oven at 200°C/400°F/gas mark 6 for about 40 minutes. Serve cold or at warm room temperature.

This dessert, which is a cross between a pudding and a custard, originates in the Piedmont region of Italy. Its flavour can be varied by substituting crushed almond brittle (praline or nougatine) or macaroons for the amaretti biscuits.

Chocolate heaven

These are irresistible little mouthfuls in which we can indulge for sheer pleasure or to reward ourselves. They are our very own 'moments of chocolate heaven' made to comfort, re-energise and relax.

Chocolate lollipops

by Omar Busi

*preparation **40 minutes** · cooking time **5 minutes** · fairly easy*

500 g/18 oz chocolate and hazelnut spread
(see page 82)
18–21 wooden lollipop sticks
12–15 small hemispherical moulds
12–15 small rectangular moulds
200 g/7 oz plain chocolate
40 ml/1½ fl oz sunflower oil
desiccated coconut, chopped pistachios

For the round iced lollies: fill the hemispherical moulds with chocolate and hazelnut spread and chill in the fridge for 10 minutes until the chocolate is firm. Unmould and press pairs of chocolate hemispheres together (using some more soft spread to stick them) while inserting a lollipop stick. Place in the freezer for 1 hour so that they freeze together and hold the stick firmly in place.

For the rectangular lollies: fill the rectangular moulds with chocolate spread and chill in the fridge for 10 minutes, until firm. Insert a lollipop stick in each one and place in the freezer for at least 1 hour, to harden and hold the stick firmly in place.

Temper the plain chocolate using one of the methods described on pages 90–95, then stir in the sunflower oil (this will make a more liquid dipping chocolate mixture). Take the frozen lollies out of the freezer and dip them briefly one by one in the chocolate coating. If wished, you can roll the coated lollies in chopped pistachios, desiccated coconut or coarsely grated plain chocolate immediately after dipping them.

Hemispherical moulds are available online or from specialist patisserie supply shops. Keep these lollies in the fridge until just before serving them.

Cocoa and rum melting moments

*preparation **20 minutes** · cooking time **15 minutes** · easy*

90 g/3 oz hazelnuts, blanched and skinned
100 g/3½ oz caster sugar
100 g/3½ oz plain flour
30 g/1 oz unsweetened cocoa powder
100 g/3½ oz butter, cut into small pieces
10 ml/scant 1 tbsp rum
pinch of salt

Grind the skinned hazelnuts with the sugar in a food processor until the nuts are fairly finely ground. Transfer to a mixing bowl and mix with the sifted plain flour and cocoa powder; add the butter.

Add the rum and a pinch of salt and combine all the ingredients with your fingertips just well enough to make the mixture smooth and homogenous. Wrap in clingfilm and chill in the fridge for 20 minutes.

Shape the mixture into about 20 small balls, slightly smaller than walnut-sized and drop them on to the work surface, so that they flatten out somewhat on the underside and are dome-shaped on top.

Transfer to a baking tray covered with baking paper and bake in a preheated oven at 180°C/350°F/gas mark 4 for 15 minutes. Allow to cool completely before storing in an airtight tin.

*The same quantity of walnuts or almonds can be substituted for hazelnuts.
A quick way of skinning nuts is to place shelled nuts in the oven to toast
them lightly and then rub the skins off with a towel or dish cloth.*

Chocolate-coated chestnut balls

*preparation **20 minutes** · cooking time **30 minutes** · easy*

1 kg/2 lb 4 oz fresh sweet chestnuts
generous pinch of salt
200 g/7 oz plain chocolate
150 g/5 oz caster sugar
40 ml/1½ fl oz Anisette liqueur or Sambuca
50 g/2 oz butter, softened
100g/3½ oz blanched, skinned and
toasted hazelnuts

Rinse the chestnuts, pierce their hard outer skins with the point of a sharp knife and boil them in a large saucepan of salted water for about 1 hour or until they are soft. Remove the hard outer skins as well as the thin inner skins (see page 118). Push them through a sieve or use a food mill with a fine-gauge disc fitted.

Chop the plain chocolate very finely and mix half of this with the chestnuts and sugar, adding the Anisette liqueur (or Sambuca) and the softened butter. Mix thoroughly and then add half the toasted and very finely chopped hazelnuts.

Mix the remaining chopped chocolate and hazelnuts in a separate bowl; spread out in a wide, shallow dish. Shape the chestnut mixture into thirty–forty 3–4-cm/1¼–1½-in balls and roll these in the chocolate and hazelnut mixture. Chill until just before serving.

For a variation on this recipe, roll the chestnut balls in desiccated coconut instead of the chocolate and hazelnut mixture.

Amaretti cakes with strawberry coulis

*preparation **40 minutes** · cooking time **20 minutes** · fairly easy*

100g/3½ oz butter, softened

2 egg yolks

100 g/3½ oz caster sugar

125 g/4½ oz amaretti biscuits, finely crushed

5 g/2 tsp unsweetened cocoa powder

30 ml/1 fl oz Marsala

100 g/3½ oz plain flour

5 g/scant 2 tsp baking powder

2 egg whites, stiffly beaten

200 g/7 oz strawberries

Beat the softened butter with a wooden spoon until pale and fluffy; stir in the egg yolks and mix thoroughly. Add the sugar, the finely crushed amaretti biscuits, the cocoa powder, Marsala and the sifted flour and baking powder. Combine thoroughly before adding the stiffly beaten egg whites, incorporating these gently but thoroughly.

Transfer the mixture to four greased individual moulds and bake in a preheated oven at 200°C/400°F/gas mark 6 for about 20 minutes.

Purée the strawberries in a food processor or blender and sieve them until you have a smooth coulis. When the amaretti cakes are cooked and have cooled completely, serve with the strawberry coulis.

You can serve vanilla-flavoured custard (see recipe on page 78) with these cakes instead of the strawberry coulis.

Rich chestnut, chocolate and orange dessert

*preparation **40 minutes** · cooking time **5 minutes** · easy*

150 g/5 oz plain chocolate, coarsely chopped
130 g/4½ oz butter, cut into small pieces
500 g/1 lb 1 oz tinned sweetened chestnut
purée or conserve
50 g/2 oz caster or icing sugar
15 g/1 tbsp brandy or 2 tbsp Marsala
1 unwaxed orange (grated rind only)
unsweetened cocoa powder, sifted

Melt the chocolate over hot water, stirring frequently. Add the butter gradually and stir with a balloon whisk to blend evenly. Mix the melted chocolate very thoroughly with the chestnut purée or conserve. Stir in the sugar, the brandy or Marsala and 1 tablespoon finely grated orange rind.

Line a 20-cm/8-in square mould smoothly with clingfilm and fill with the mixture. Smooth the top with a palette knife dipped in cold water and chill in the fridge for at least 12 hours. Four–six small, round or hexagonal individual moulds can also be used.

Unmould just before serving; sprinkle with the sifted cocoa powder and decorate with whole marrons glacés and/or sugared or caramelised almonds. Slice and serve.

Marron (chestnut) conserve is available online and from specialised retailers.
If it is rum-flavoured, substitute rum for brandy in this recipe. If tinned,
sweetened, vanilla-flavoured chestnut purée is used, add rum or brandy.
Serve with whipped cream if wished.

Chocolate cornets

by Omar Busi

*preparation **40 minutes** · cooking time **10 minutes** · easy*

700 g/1½ lb gianduia or praline chocolate
300 g/10 oz milk chocolate, coarsely chopped
400 ml/14 fl oz full-cream milk
100 ml/3½ fl oz liquid glucose
150 g/5 oz butter, softened
50 mini ice cream cornets (moulded wafer type)
100 g/3½ oz plain chocolate
1 tbsp peanut oil or sunflower oil

To decorate
chopped hazelnuts, crumbled amaretti biscuits
and marshmallow sprinkles

Break the gianduia or praline chocolate into small pieces and place in a bowl with the milk chocolate. Heat the milk and liquid glucose to just below boiling point and pour over all the chocolate pieces. Mix the chocolate and milk well until the chocolate has melted and the mixture is smooth and glossy. Stir in the butter. Pour this ganache out into a shallow dish and chill in the fridge, stirring frequently as it gradually thickens.

Fill a piping bag fitted with a fluted nozzle with the thick ganache and pipe swirls of ganache ending in soft peaks into the top of each ice cream cone. Chill in the fridge, placed upright if possible, until completely set.

Temper the plain chocolate using any of the methods on pages 90–95and add the sunflower oil to keep the chocolate fluid for dipping. Dip the whole ice cream cornets one by one in the chocolate and, before the chocolate hardens totally, sprinkle the tops with your choice of decoration. Chill until just before serving.

These mini cornets can be bought from some ice cream parlours or from specialist suppliers (shops or online). If you cannot buy gianduia or praline chocolate, use 700 g/1 lb 8 oz milk chocolate instead, mixed with 300 g/10 oz plain chocolate.

Brandy soft-centre chocolates

*preparation **40 minutes** · cooking time **10 minutes** · advanced*

250 g/9 oz double cream
60 g/generous 2 oz butter
250 g/9 oz milk chocolate, coarsely chopped
100 ml/3½ fl oz brandy (e.g. Armagnac)

To coat and decorate
200 g/7 oz plain chocolate or
couverture, coarsely chopped
60 g/2 oz milk chocolate, coarsely chopped

Heat the cream with the butter to boiling point, then pour into a stainless steel bowl, preferably with a pouring lip. Add the chopped milk chocolate and the brandy. Whisk continuously with a balloon whisk until all the chocolate has melted and the ingredients are smoothly blended. Pour into about 30 little chocolate moulds. Allow to cool before chilling in the fridge for at least 2 hours.

Melt the plain chocolate or couverture for the coating over hot water. When the chocolate in the moulds is hard and chilled, take them out of their little moulds and place them on a cake rack or grid. Pour the melted chocolate evenly and carefully over them; allow to cool then return them to the fridge to set hard.

Decorate the coated chocolates: melt the milk chocolate over hot water or in the microwave. Pour it into a piping bag fitted with a very small aperture plain nozzle. Pipe two milk chocolate strips near one end of each chocolate, allow to set and then serve.

If you do not have a piping bag and nozzle, cut out a fairly large triangle of greaseproof paper, pull one corner round to overlap the other and form a cone, fold over the top to secure and snip off the tip of the pointed cone. Fill with the melted chocolate and pipe.

Three-tone chocolates

by Omar Busi

*preparation **40 minutes** · easy*

For the white chocolate layer
500 g/1 lb 1oz white chocolate
250 g/9 oz hazelnut or almond paste
30 g/1 oz cocoa butter

For the milk chocolate layer
500 g/1 lb 1 oz milk chocolate
250 g/9 oz hazelnut or almond paste
15 g/½ oz cocoa butter

For the plain chocolate layer
500 g/1 lb 1 oz plain chocolate
275 g/10 oz hazelnut or almond paste

Prepare each type and shade of chocolate mixture in separate bowls by combining the hazelnut or almond paste with the tempered chocolate (see pages 90–95 for methods) and then adding the cocoa butter when required. Fill a piping bag with the white chocolate mixture and pipe a layer of this into 35–40 hemispherical moulds in a flexipan or silicone tray for making chocolates.

Wait until this first layer has cooled, then chill in the fridge for 5 minutes; repeat this piping operation with the milk chocolate mixture in a clean piping bag; wait until this layer has set, then chill in the fridge as before; finally fill the moulds with the last, plain chocolate layer in the same way. Allow to become firm, chill and then unmould the chocolates carefully.

If you cannot buy hazelnut paste, make it yourself by grinding 250 g/9 oz blanched, skinned hazelnuts in a food processor, then knead and roll out the ground hazelnuts until you have a marzipan-type paste. In hot weather it is advisable to add 15 g/½ oz cocoa butter to the milk chocolate and 30 g/1 oz to the white chocolate to stabilise it.

Limoncello and white chocolate mousse

*preparation **30 minutes** • cooking time **5 minutes** • easy*

10 g/scant ½ oz leaf gelatine
170 g/6 oz white chocolate
3 egg yolks
70 g/2½ oz caster sugar
scant 3 egg whites
30 ml/1 fl oz Limoncello liqueur
1 unwaxed lemon (grated rind only)
500 ml/18 fl oz whipping cream

To decorate
200 g/7 oz blueberries

Soak the gelatine in cold water. Melt the white chocolate over hot water. Whisk the egg yolks with the sugar in a mixing bowl until pale and creamy. Add the melted white chocolate and stir well.

Whisk the egg whites until stiff and fold into the chocolate mixture. Heat the Limoncello liqueur in a small saucepan and remove from the heat. Squeeze any excess moisture out of the leaf gelatine and add to the hot Limoncello to melt completely. Stir well.

Add the gelatine and Limoncello mixture to the chocolate mixture, stir well, adding the lemon rind. Whip the cream stiffly and fold into the chocolate mixture. Spoon into four–six individual glass dishes containing some blueberries and chill for at least 5 hours.

You can vary this recipe by using plain chocolate instead of white and flavour it with an orange liqueur instead of the Limoncello.

Chocolate 'salami'

preparation **30 minutes** · *easy*

100 g/3½ oz butter, softened
100 g/3½ oz caster sugar
1 egg yolk
½ egg white
50 g/2 oz unsweetened cocoa powder
150 g/5 oz Petit Beurre or Rich Tea biscuits
15 ml/1 tbsp dry Marsala
35 ml/2½ tbsp Navy rum

Beat the butter and sugar in a mixing bowl until pale and creamy; beat in the egg yolk, followed by the egg white and the sifted cocoa powder. Stir in the very finely crushed biscuits and moisten by adding a few drops of Marsala and rum at a time until you have added the quantity required.

Work the mixture well until it sticks together, then shape into a very thick sausage shape and wrap in waxed paper or greaseproof paper. Chill in the fridge for 4 hours. Serve cold, cut into about 20 fairly thick slices.

To give the chocolate salami a different flavour and texture, add approximately 200 g/7 oz very finely chopped best-quality hazelnuts to the mixture and moisten with an orange liqueur instead of the rum and Marsala.

Black and white millefeuille

*preparation **25 minutes** · cooking time **20 minutes** · easy*

3 egg yolks
150 g/5 oz caster sugar
80 g/3 oz plain flour
500 ml/18 fl oz full-cream milk
1 unwaxed lemon (grated rind only)
1 vanilla pod
300 g/10 oz plain chocolate
500 ml/18 fl oz double cream
1 x 200-g/7-oz packet
ready-rolled all-butter puff pastry

Whisk the egg yolks with 100 g/3½ oz of the caster sugar in a heatproof mixing bowl until pale and fluffy; whisk in the sifted flour a little at a time, alternating with small quantities of the milk, followed by a scant 1 teaspoon of finely grated lemon rind and the seeds from the vanilla pod (split the pod in half lengthways and, using a smooth-bladed knife, scrape out the seeds).

Place the mixing bowl over hot water or transfer the mixture to the top of a large double-boiler and cook gently, stirring continuously, until the confectioner's custard or pastry cream thickens. Remove from the heat and stir until it has cooled a little.

Melt the chocolate over hot water. Heat 300 ml/10 fl oz of the cream and then whisk it into the melted chocolate in a thin stream. The mixture should be very smooth. Beat the remaining cream until stiff and stir in the remaining sugar. Fold into the mixture.

Bake the puff pastry sheet as instructed on the packet and allow to cool. Cut to form a rectangle, bake and separate the layers horizontally in half. Place one layer of pastry on a wide serving plate; cover with a layer of the confectioner's custard; cover this with another layer of puff pastry and top with the chocolate mixture. Decorate by piping extra whipped cream on top if wished, and serve. This should make about 4–6 servings.

You can buy ready-rolled, all-butter frozen puff pastry and make your own freshly baked pastry.

Chocolate crème brûlée

*preparation **25 minutes** · cooking time **15 minutes** · easy*

2 egg yolks
40 g/1½ oz caster sugar
20 g/2 tbsp potato flour or cornflour
100 ml/3½ fl oz full-cream milk, warmed
200 ml/7 fl oz double cream or
clotted cream, warmed
80 g/3 oz plain chocolate
15–30 g/½–1 oz cane sugar
(golden or muscovado)

Whisk the egg yolks with the caster sugar and the potato flour or cornflour in a heatproof mixing bowl, then gradually whisk in the lukewarm milk and the lukewarm cream. Continue heating and stirring over hot (not boiling) water, until quite thick. Remove from the heat.

Chop the chocolate coarsely and stir it into the hot custard until it has completely melted. Pour this custard into six individual ramekins or small soufflé dishes and then leave to cool.

Chill the custards in the fridge until just before serving. Sprinkle their surfaces with the cane sugar and place the ramekin dishes in a grill pan under a very hot grill. The sugar should melt and caramelise. Serve at once.

A very good technique for caramelising the sugar topping of the custards is to place the dishes in a roasting pan or grill pan and add sufficient cold or iced water to come three quarters of the way up the sides of the dishes. The heat will therefore be concentrated on the sugar topping and the custard below will stay cool.

Hazelnut swirls

*preparation **25 minutes** · cooking time **10 minutes** · easy*

150 g/5 oz milk chocolate
60 g/2 oz chocolate and hazelnut spread
(see page 82)
20 ml/generous 1 tbsp Cointreau
100 g/3½ oz butter, softened
icing or caster sugar

Melt the chocolate over hot water or in the microwave. Heat 150 ml/5 fl oz water in a saucepan with the chocolate and hazelnut spread (see recipe on page 82) and the Cointreau, stirring well. As soon as it nears boiling point, remove from the heat and pour into the melted chocolate, whisking continuously with a balloon whisk; stir in the butter. Continue stirring until the mixture is smooth and homogenous. Chill in the fridge for at least 20 minutes.

Fill a piping bag fitted with a fluted nozzle with the chocolate mixture. Cover a baking tray with baking paper and pipe about 20 small swirls of mixture on to this. Chill in the fridge for 2 hours to solidify.

Dust the chocolate swirls liberally with sifted icing sugar or sprinkle with caster sugar. Chill in the fridge until just before serving.

The practical way of serving these swirls is to put them in little fluted paper cases so that your guests will not get sugar all over their hands.

Individual tiramisù with chocolate

*preparation **40 minutes** · cooking time **20 minutes** · easy*

8 sponge fingers
100 ml/3½ fl oz egg liqueur (e.g. Advocaat)
80 g/3 oz milk chocolate
80 g/3 oz double cream
4 egg yolks
25 g/1 oz caster sugar
15 ml/1 tbsp sweet Marsala
60 g/2 oz mascarpone

To decorate
20 g/scant 1 oz instant coffee granules

Cut the sponge fingers in half and dip them in the egg liqueur; place them vertically around the insides of four glass tumblers so that their cut ends rest on the bottom of each glass. Melt the chocolate with the cream in the microwave or over hot water; stir, and pour into the glasses while still warm.

Whisk the egg yolks and the sugar in a mixing bowl placed over hot water, continue whisking while the mixture is warmed by the steam and it has tripled in volume. Add the Marsala and continue whisking briefly.

Remove from the heat and plunge the bottom of the bowl into iced water to halt the cooking process. Fold the mascarpone into the mixture and spoon into the glasses. Allow to stand for five minutes before sprinkling some coffee granules over the top. Serve with wafer biscuits if wished.

Mascarpone cheese goes very well with chocolate: both are high in fat content and so blend very agreeably together.

Pear frappé with vanilla foam

*preparation **20 minutes** · cooking time **5 minutes** · easy*

200 ml/7 fl oz full-cream milk
100 g/3½ oz milk chocolate,
coarsely chopped
2 sweet, ripe pears
15 g/½ oz cane sugar

For the vanilla foam
100 ml/3½ fl oz whipping cream
20 g/scant 1 oz vanilla sugar (see page 20)
crushed ice

Heat the milk (do not allow to boil) and melt the chocolate in it. Stir well and leave to cool. Peel the pears, remove the cores and cut into small pieces.

Place the pears in a food processor or blender with the cane sugar and process until you have a smooth purée. Add the milk and chocolate mixture and process (add a little double cream if wished for a creamier taste).

Pour this mixture into four tall glass tumblers. Wash the food processor or blender and place five ice cubes in it with the cream and vanilla sugar. Process at full speed and use as a frothy topping for the pear and chocolate mixture in the tumblers.

For a stronger flavour, cut the peeled and cored pears in half, sprinkle them with cane sugar, chestnut honey and a pinch of ground star anise. Cook the pears in the oven in a dish covered with greaseproof paper at 200°C/400°F/gas mark 6 for 20 minutes. As soon as they are cooked, liquidise them and follow the recipe above.

Amaretto, chocolate and pistachio truffles

*preparation **20 minutes** · cooking time **10 minutes** · easy*

200 g/7 oz full-cream milk
2–3 tbsp Amaretto liqueur
400 g/14 oz sweet yeast cake
(e.g. the Italian pandoro)
50 g/2 oz amaretti biscuits
80 g/3oz plain chocolate
70 ml/2½ oz double cream

To decorate
60 g/2 oz shelled and skinned pistachios
20 g/scant 1 oz flaked almonds

Mix the milk with two to three tablespoons of the Amaretto liqueur; cut the sweet yeast cake of your choice into large slices and moisten these in the flavoured milk. Leave to soak for 5 minutes, then squeeze out all excess moisture. Mix the moistened cake well with the finely crushed amaretti biscuits: the mixture should be firm and cohesive. Taking a small quantity at a time, roll into about 30 balls a little smaller than a walnut. Place on a plate and cover with clingfilm; chill in the fridge to make them very firm.

Chop the chocolate and melt it with the cream over hot water or in the microwave; stir well and allow to cool. Chop the pistachios finely and toast the flaked almonds lightly in the oven.

Place the chilled balls on a rack; transfer the melted chocolate mixture to a piping bag (you can make your own by wrapping two points of a triangle of greaseproof paper around one another, forming a cone, and snipping off the tip) and cover the balls with chocolate (or you can simply spoon the melted chocolate over them with a teaspoon). Sprinkle with the chopped pistachios and flaked almonds. Chill until needed.

Almost any sweet yeast bread or cake can be used for this recipe, such as brioche or plain panettone.

Soft chocolate cubes with fresh strawberries

*preparation **30 minutes** • cooking time **25 minutes** • easy*

75 g/2½ oz almonds, blanched and skinned
100 g/3½ oz milk chocolate
50 g/2 oz plain chocolate
75 g/2½ butter, softened
75 g/2½ oz caster sugar
15 ml/1 tbsp brandy
2 eggs
100 g/3½ oz mascarpone
40 g/1½ oz plain flour
10 g/1 tbsp potato flour or cornflour

To decorate
200 g/7 oz strawberries
50 g/2 oz white chocolate

Toast the almonds lightly in the oven at 170°C/325°F/gas mark 3 and then chop them finely in a food processor. Melt both the milk and plain chocolate together over hot water or in the microwave.

Whisk the butter and sugar with a hand-held electric whisk until pale and fluffy; add the melted chocolate, the brandy, the beaten eggs and, lastly, the mascarpone. Stir in the chopped almonds. Sift in the plain flour with the potato flour or cornflour and stir in well. Pour this mixture into about 30 little rectangular cake moulds. Bake in a preheated oven at 180°C/350°F/gas mark 4 for 20 minutes, then take out and leave to cool.

Rinse and hull the strawberries and cut them in half. Melt the white chocolate and allow it to cool to lukewarm. Turn out the cakes and cut them into cubes; spoon a little white chocolate on top of each cube and place a half strawberry on top. Serve when cold.

You can vary this recipe by using the same quantity of raspberries or blackberries instead of strawberries.

Hazelnut praline chocolates

*preparation **30 minutes** · cooking time **15 minutes** · easy*

100 g/3½ oz hazelnuts, blanched and skinned
150 g/5 oz milk chocolate
40 ml/1½ fl oz double cream,
at room temperature

Toast the hazelnuts lightly in the oven at 170°C/325°F/gas mark 3 or in a non-stick frying pan. Allow them to cool before chopping them coarsely. Melt two thirds of the chocolate over hot water or in the microwave and when this first batch has completely melted, add the remaining one third of the chocolate and allow to melt.

Add the chopped hazelnuts and pour in the cream in a thin stream while stirring thoroughly. Pour into 25–30 small chocolate moulds or into a single square or rectangular mould (you can cut the chocolate into squares when it has set).

Chill the chocolates, covered with clingfilm, in the fridge. Serve in little paper cases.

These chocolates are also delicious when made with walnuts or skinned almonds, following exactly the same method.

Bain-marie This method of warming or cooking by means of indirect heat gives the cook greater control over very delicate ingredients. When setting up a *bain-marie*, the ingredients to be processed are placed in a bowl; a pan or baking tray of a size and shape that will accommodate the first comfortably and securely is then part-filled with boiling water. The bowl is then placed over or in the pan or baking tray containing the hot water, which in turn is put directly on a hob burner or in the oven. The heat keeps the water simmering and warmth is conducted into the food, a method that is both gentle and easily controllable. The technique is slow, but indispensable to pastry cooks and confectioners, especially when working with chocolate and in the preparation of puddings, custards, crème caramels and some jams.

Beating Processing an ingredient or mixture to make it softer and lighter, often making it increase considerably in volume, either with or without gentle indirect heat beneath it.

Bowls Stainless steel bowls are an excellent choice, with or without handles. When beating egg mixtures, especially egg whites, a copper hemispherical bowl is the professional's choice. Eggs react adversely to aluminium.

Butter Butter can be warmed in the microwave on a low setting for 10 seconds, then worked or 'creamed' with a spatula to make it light and soft. Alternatively, butter can be left at warm room temperature until it acquires a spreadable consistency and can then be beaten or creamed.

Caramelising Sugar is heated until it melts and caramelises. The colour can range from golden to dark brown, depending on how long it is heated; it develops an increasingly pronounced, rich flavour.

Cornflour Used to thicken sauces and for making desserts and cakes. Potato flour can be used instead.

Coulis A sauce of fruit purée. When the fruit is cooked uncovered much of the water content evaporates.

Dust or dredge The use of a sifter or sieve to sprinkle powdery substances such as flour, cornflour or icing sugar evenly over foods in course of preparation and, in the case of icing sugar and cocoa powder, as a finishing touch when they are cooked.

Emulsion Two or more substances of different densities are beaten with a whisk until they apparently blend together (often temporarily) into a homogenous liquid.

Essences Used in patisserie to flavour and add aroma to mixtures or confections, these are usually of plant origin (orange, mint, ginger), extracted by a process of maceration(definition follows) or distillation and preserved in an alcoholic solution.

Flour The use of a flour sifter to sprinkle a thin covering of flour over a surface to prevent ingredients from sticking to it when they are handled or rolled out.

Fold Adding ingredients to whisked or beaten mixtures very gently to avoid crushing the air out of them while incorporating them evenly and thoroughly.

Food mixers and processors These time- and labour-saving electric appliances are no longer confined to professional kitchens. They halve the time needed to whisk or otherwise process ingredients and mixtures, guaranteeing satisfactory results.

Gelatine An odourless, tasteless gelling agent, very pale beige in colour. Soak leaf gelatine in cold water for a few minutes to soften before melting. Also available in powdered form.

Glaze Warmed, sieved jam, or fruit juice with a gelling agent dissolved in it; applied before or after cooking to enhance the appearance of fruit flans and other confections.

Grease To cover a baking receptacle with a thin layer of unsalted butter which is then usually dusted with flour, or with sugar which will caramelise on the sides and edges of sweet baked goods.

Hand blender This electric utensil is very practical and easy to use, the revolving components are immersed in the substance to be emulsified or blended.

Hand-held electric whisk This appliance is also lowered directly into the receptacle containing the food to be processed. Various attachments can be inserted into the sockets in the lower end of the tube containing the powerful motor depending on whether the ingredient has to be mixed, crushed, puréed or chopped. A special three-bladed cutting attachment revolves at thousands of revolutions per minute.

Macerate Aromatic substances such as spices or citrus peels are left to soak for some time in a sugar syrup or a wine-based liqueur or spirit and impart their flavour and aroma to the macerating liquid.

Melt Warming and liquefying a solid substance such as butter or chocolate in a *bain-marie* (over hot water) or in the microwave on a low setting to avoid denaturing the ingredient.

Nozzle These come in various shapes (round, star, scroll and petal) and sizes, in stainless steel or plastic. They are inserted into piping bags and used to pipe fillings and decorations.

Paper cases (fluted) These are used as containers for biscuits, cakes and confectionery, especially by commercial confectioners.

Pasta-rolling machine Domestic machine for rolling out pastry or pasta to various thicknesses and sizes. Manually operated and electrically powered machines are an alternative to the more traditional rolling pin.

Pastry board or table These provide a perfectly level and smooth wooden surface for mixing, kneading and rolling out pastry and pasta. They should be kept in a dry place at a constant temperature when not in use to prevent the wood warping.

Pastry cutter These utensils come in various shapes and sizes, have no base and are usually made of tinned steel or plastic. They are used to cut home-made pastry, biscuit dough and other mixtures.

Piping bag or forcing bag A cone-shaped bag made of plastic or material with a hole in the pointed end to take the nozzle and filled with the creams, fillings, custards and icings to be piped for a decorative effect on a wide range of culinary preparations.

Potato flour A culinary starch extracted from potatoes. This flour is very fine indeed and is used as an alternative or in addition to wheat flour for very light preparations or to make mixtures with very high fat, egg and sugar contents more friable and delicate. It is also ideal for binding or thickening creamy desserts, sauces and custards.

Reduce Boiling a substance in an uncovered receptacle, making a sauce or liquid thicker and more concentrated through evaporation.

Rolling out Thicknesses of short pastry, puff pastry and biscuit dough are usually specified when instructions call for rolling out mixtures with a rolling pin or with a machine.

Sieve (Chinois) Often called a conical sieve; used to separate liquids from solids and filter out thicker ingredients from thinner ones. Varying sizes are available, made of tinned steel, stainless steel or nylon, with coarser or finer meshes depending on their use. Some sieves manufactured in the Far East have meshes of thread-like woven bamboo strips; they are fragile but ideal for straining foods that react adversely if they come into contact with metal. Sieves need careful handling and cleaning.

Sift Shaking flour, icing sugar etc. in a sifter or sieve gets rid of any lumps and also introduces air into mixtures to make them lighter.

Silpat Sheets or 'mats' which prevent food sticking to baking ware. They can be used at temperatures ranging from -40ºC/-40ºF to 280ºC/536ºF and can also be used for deep-freezing foods.

Tempering A technique for processing chocolate which involves melting chocolate at a specific temperature, then cooling it down to 31°C/87.8°F after which it can be used for a variety of purposes, mainly decorative. Respecting the correct temperatures is crucial to achieving a successful outcome, resulting in chocolate that has an excellent consistency and colour.

Thicken A thickening agent is added to a mixture or to a sauce to bind it and/or make it thicker. This can be done with a variety of mixtures.

Toasting Heating nuts in the oven or in a non-stick pan until pale golden brown results in partial evaporation of their water content and increased crunchiness.

Vanilla pod This flavouring comes from a plant native to tropical regions of the Americas. Pods are cured for approximately one year; they are used whole to flavour sweet sauces and syrups or split lengthwise in half and the seeds scraped out and used for flavouring.

Well When flour is sifted in a mound on to a work surface, pastry board or into a large mixing bowl, a well or depression is made in the centre in which the ingredients to be worked into the flour are placed.

Whisk Utensil used to introduce air into a substance, making it much lighter. Balloon whisks are usually made of stainless steel, with a varying number of overlapping wires, depending on their use.

Whisking Introducing air and greatly increasing volume. For best results when whisking egg whites it is best to start off slowly and gradually increase the speed of whisking: they will remain firm for longer.

About the Authors

Francesca Badi, cookery editor for the Italian publisher Food Editore, is the co-ordinator of various recipe books and a title on wine and gastronomy. She has edited a number of titles for Food Editore, published in Italy, including *Bread*, *School of Cookery* and *Home-made Dishes*.

Omar Busi is a young but well-established master pâtissier. He has won many prizes, both in Italy and in other countries, for his excellent chocolate-based creations. Apart from running a chocolate business in Pieve di Centro (Bologna), he also teaches and organises several pâtisserie courses. He is a founder member of the Italian chocolatiers' organisation CiocchinBo – Maestri Cioccolatieri Associati, which exhibits at the world-famous annual Cioccoshow in Bologna.

The tables below are only approximate and are meant to be used as a guide only.

Approximate American/European conversions

	USA	Metric	Imperial
brown sugar	1 cup	170 g	6 oz
butter	1 stick	115 g	4 oz
butter/margarine/lard	1 cup	225 g	8 oz
caster and granulated sugar	2 level tablespoons	30 g	1 oz
caster and granulated sugar	1 cup	225 g	8 oz
currants	1 cup	140 g	5 oz
flour	1 cup	140 g	5 oz
golden syrup	1 cup	350 g	12 oz
ground almonds	1 cup	115 g	4 oz
sultanas/raisins	1 cup	200 g	7 oz

Approximate American/ European conversions

American	European
1 teaspoon	1 teaspoon/5 ml
½ fl oz	1 tablespoon/ ½ fl oz/15 ml
¼ cup	4 tablespoons/2 fl oz/50 ml
½ cup plus 2 tablespoons	¼ pint/5 fl oz/150 ml
1¼ cups	½ pint/10 fl oz/300 ml
1 pint/16 fl oz	1 pint/20 fl oz/600 ml
2½ pints (5 cups)	1.2 litres/2 pints
10 pints	4.5 litres/8 pints

Oven temperatures

American	Celsius	Fahrenheit	Gas Mark
Cool	130	250	½
Very slow	140	275	1
Slow	150	300	2
Moderate	160	320	3
Moderate	180	350	4
Moderately hot	190	375	5
Fairly hot	200	400	6
Hot	220	425	7
Very hot	230	450	8
Extremely hot	240	475	9

Liquid measures

Imperial	ml	fl oz
1 teaspoon	5	
2 tablespoons	30	
4 tablespoons	60	
¼ pint/1 gill	150	5
⅓ pint	200	7
½ pint	300	10
¾ pint	425	15
1 pint	600	20
1¾ pints	1000 (1 litre)	35

Other useful measurements

Measurement	Metric	Imperial
1 American cup	225 ml	8 fl oz
1 egg, size 3	50 ml	2 fl oz
1 egg white	30 ml	1 fl oz
1 rounded tablespoon flour	30 g	1 oz
1 rounded tablespoon cornflour	30 g	1 oz
1 rounded tablespoon caster sugar	30 g	1 oz
2 level teaspoons gelatine	10 g	¼ oz